YOUR recipe could appear in our next cookbook!

Share your tried & true family favorites with us instantly at
www.gooseberrypatch.com

If you'd rather jot 'em down by hand, just mail this form to...
Gooseberry Patch • Cookbooks – Call for Recipes
PO Box 812 • Columbus, OH 43216-0812

If your recipe is selected for a book, you'll receive a FREE copy!

Please share only your original recipes or those that you have made your own over the years.

Recipe Name:

Number of Servings:

Any fond memories about this recipe? Special touches you like to add or handy shortcuts?

Ingredients (include specific measurements):

Instructions (continue on back if needed):

Special Code: **cookbookspage**

Over ↗

Extra space for recipe if needed:

Tell us about yourself...

Your complete contact information is needed so that we can send you your FREE cookbook, if your recipe is published. Phone numbers and email addresses are kept private and will only be used if we have questions about your recipe.

Name:

Address:

City: State: Zip:

Email:

Daytime Phone:

Thank you! Vickie & Jo Ann

· SHORTCUTS TO ·
Grandma's Best
· RECIPES ·

255 recipes for favorite comfort foods,
made easy with store-bought shortcuts.

Gooseberry Patch

An imprint of Globe Pequot
64 South Main Street
Essex, CT 06426

www.gooseberrypatch.com

1•800•854•6673

Do you have a tried & true recipe...

tip, craft or memory that you'd like to see featured in
a **Gooseberry Patch** cookbook? Visit our website at
www.gooseberrypatch.com and follow the
easy steps to submit your favorite family recipe.
Or send them to us at:

Gooseberry Patch
PO Box 812
Columbus, OH 43216-0812

Don't forget to include the number of servings your recipe makes,
plus your name, address, phone number and email address. If we
select your recipe, your name will appear right along with it...
and you'll receive a **FREE** copy of the book!

Contents

Dedication

To families everywhere who cherish their time spent together, sharing good food.

Appreciation

Thanks to everyone who shared your best recipes for those days when you're short on time, but long on love.

Busy-Day Breakfast Shortcusts

Applesauce Pancakes

Sue Klapper
Muskego, WI

My dad used to make apple pancakes when I was a child. I think of him whenever I make them myself. Be sure to choose "complete" pancake mix...you won't need to add any milk or egg!

1 c. complete pancake mix
1 T. sugar
1 t. cinnamon
3/4 c. water

1/3 c. applesauce
Optional: additional applesauce,
    cinnamon-sugar

In a bowl, combine pancake mix, sugar and cinnamon; mix well. Add water and applesauce; whisk together until fairly smooth. Some lumps will remain. Spray a non-stick griddle with non-stick vegetable spray. Add batter to hot griddle by 1/4 cupfuls. Cook until pancakes are golden on the bottom and surface is bubbly. Turn and cook until golden on the other side. Serve pancakes topped with applesauce and cinnamon-sugar, as desired. Makes 8 pancakes.

Set the breakfast table the night before...you may even get
the kids to help you. In the morning, you can enjoy
a relaxed breakfast together.

Busy-Day Breakfast Shortcuts

Farmers' Break-of-Day Casserole

Janice Curtis
Yucaipa, CA

I've made this tasty casserole many times. It's great for feeding your family or for carrying to a potluck.

6 c. frozen shredded hashbrowns
2 c. cooked ham, diced
1/2 c. green onions, sliced
8-oz. pkg. shredded Cheddar
  cheese, divided

8 eggs, beaten
2 5-oz. cans evaporated milk

Spread hashbrowns evenly in a greased 13"x9" baking pan. Layer with ham, onions and 1-1/2 cups cheese; set aside. In a large bowl, whisk together eggs and evaporated milk; pour over hashbrown mixture. Top with remaining cheese. Bake, uncovered, at 350 degrees for 45 to 55 minutes, until hot and bubbly. Let stand for several minutes before cutting into squares. Makes 8 servings.

A batter bowl with a pouring spout and a handle is super-handy for whisking eggs and so many more kitchen tasks. When not in use, fill it with shiny red apples to double as a casual centerpiece.

Potato, Sausage & Egg
Breakfast Casserole

Carrie O'Shea
Marina del Rey, CA

A very adaptable recipe! Try it with southwestern-style liquid egg substitute, or add a big spoonful of salsa and your favorite cheese.

16-oz. container liquid egg
   substitute, or 8 eggs, beaten
1/2 c. milk
seasoning salt and pepper
   to taste
4 frozen brown & serve pork
   sausage links, sliced

2 c. refrigerated shredded
   hashbrown potatoes
1/2 c. red pepper, diced
1/2 c. shredded sharp Cheddar
   cheese

In a large bowl, combine eggs, milk, seasoning salt and pepper; whisk well. Stir in remaining ingredients. Pour mixture into a buttered 8"x8" glass baking pan. Bake, uncovered, at 350 degrees for 45 minutes, or until eggs are set and a knife tip inserted in the center comes out clean. Cool slightly before serving. Serves 4.

Eggs and potatoes are tasty with catsup, but to really
wake everyone up at breakfast time, add some
spicy salsa or hot pepper sauce!

Busy-Day Breakfast Shortcuts

Favorite Amish Baked Oatmeal
Rachelle Bohner
Harrisburg, PA

I adapted this recipe from one I found in an Amish cookbook. It is always a hit with my family, church members and co-workers at the office. It's easy to make and I usually have all the ingredients on hand. When I make it for work, everyone runs for the kitchen as soon as they find out it's there!

1/2 c. brown sugar, packed
1/4 c. sugar
1/2 c. oil
2 eggs, beaten
1 to 2 T. vanilla extract

1 c. milk
3 c. old-fashioned oats, uncooked
2 t. baking powder

Mix together all ingredients in a bowl. Pour into a lightly greased 13"x9" baking pan. Bake, uncovered, at 350 degrees for 30 to 40 minutes. Makes 8 to 14 servings.

Variations: Add 1/2 to one cup fruit of your choice. Diced apples are my go-to for this recipe...sliced bananas, fresh blueberries, dried cranberries and even chocolate chips are all delicious too.

Keep a few cans of evaporated milk in the pantry. You can use it as a substitute when you're out of whole milk or half-and-half in just about any kind of recipe.

Ham & Cheese Breakfast Sandwiches

Jennie Gist
Gooseberry Patch

A quick, fun breakfast before everyone heads out to work and school. You'll have two biscuits left over...top with butter and serve, for anyone who's still hungry. Delicious with crumbled bacon too.

16.3-oz. tube refrigerated jumbo
    flaky biscuits
6 eggs
2 T. milk

salt and pepper to taste
1/2 c. deli baked ham, chopped
1 c. shredded Cheddar cheese

Bake biscuits according to package directions; set aside to cool. Meanwhile, in a large bowl, whisk together eggs, milk, salt and pepper; fold in ham. Pour egg mixture into a greased 8"x8" baking pan. Bake at 350 degrees for 24 minutes, or until eggs are set and a knife tip inserted in the center comes out clean. Sprinkle with cheese; return to oven until cheese is melted. Cut baked eggs into 6 squares. Split biscuits; fill each with an egg square and serve. Makes 6 sandwiches.

If kids aren't in the mood for traditional breakfast foods, let 'em be creative! A peanut butter sandwich, a slice of leftover pizza or a helping of last night's taco casserole will get their day off to a good start. Add a glass of milk or orange juice for a balanced meal.

Busy-Day Breakfast Shortcuts

Waffle Maker Hashbrowns

Beckie Apple
Grannis, AR

Since I've retired, I really enjoy experimenting with new recipes. This one using my waffle maker is really a keeper!

2 c. frozen shredded hashbrown
    potatoes, thawed
salt and pepper to taste

3 green onions, thinly sliced
1/2 c. real bacon bits
1 c. shredded Cheddar cheese

Spray a waffle iron with non-stick vegetable spray and preheat until hot. Squeeze out any excess moisture from hashbrowns; spread evenly on waffle iron. Lightly season with salt and pepper; sprinkle with onions, bacon bits and cheese. Close waffle iron and cook for 2 to 3 minutes, until crisp and golden. Remove to a serving plate; cut into 4 squares and serve hot. Makes 4 servings.

For perfect hard-boiled eggs every time, cover eggs with water in a saucepan; bring to a rolling boil. Remove pan from heat, cover and let stand for 18 to 20 minutes. Immediately plunge eggs into ice water and peel. Keep a few in the fridge for quick snacks!

Overnight Oats in a Jar

Lisa Gowen
Saint Charles, MO

I like to fix these on Sunday afternoon, then I am ready to go each morning with a good breakfast before work, plus a bonus serving for Saturday. Your healthy breakfast will be ready for you before you head out!

1/2 c. quick-cooking oats, uncooked
1/2 c. plain Greek yogurt
1 t. chia seeds

1 t. chopped pecans, or to taste
1-pint canning jar with lid
Optional: cinnamon to taste
1/2 c. almond milk or dairy milk

Layer oats, yogurt, chia seeds and pecans evenly in jar. Add a sprinkle of cinnamon, if desired. Add milk; stir well to combine. Close jar with lid. Refrigerate overnight before serving. Makes one serving.

When you rise in the morning, form a resolution
to make the day a happy one for a fellow creature.

–Sydney Smith

Gingerbread Pancakes

*Kathy Grashoff
Fort Wayne, IN*

Why save gingerbread just for the holidays? Serve with maple syrup...a dollop of whipped cream would be delicious, too! Use "complete" pancake mix, no milk or egg added.

2 c. complete pancake mix	1/2 t. ground ginger
4 t. molasses	1/8 t. ground cloves
1/2 t. cinnamon	1-1/2 c. water

In a large bowl, combine pancake mix, molasses and spices; mix well. Add water and stir just until moistened. Add batter by 1/4 cupfuls onto a greased hot griddle. Cook until bubbles form on top; turn over and cook until golden. Makes 12 pancakes.

Extra pancakes and waffles can be frozen up to a month in plastic freezer bags. Reheat them in a toaster for a quick homestyle breakfast on busy weekdays.

Eggs, Biscuits & Gravy

Sue Morrison
Blue Springs, MO

This is a different way to serve a hot breakfast...my family loves it! You can double it or make any amount you want for a larger group. Eggs can be boiled up ahead of time...if you prefer, serve on slices of buttered toast instead of biscuits. It really goes together fast!

6-oz. tube refrigerated biscuits
4 eggs, hard-boiled, peeled
   and halved

2-3/4 oz. pkg. peppered white
   country gravy mix
salt and pepper to taste

Bake biscuits according to package directions. Meanwhile, separate egg yolks from whites. Chop egg whites and set aside in a bowl. Grate egg yolks; set aside in another bowl. Prepare gravy according to package instructions. Add chopped egg whites to gravy and mix gently. On each of 4 to 5 warmed plates, place a split biscuit. Divide gravy evenly among biscuits; sprinkle evenly with grated egg yolk. Season with salt and pepper and serve. Makes 4 to 5 servings.

The smell of buttered toast simply talked to Toad,
and with no uncertain voice; talked of warm kitchens,
of breakfasts on bright frosty mornings...
–Kenneth Grahame

Busy-Day Breakfast Shortcuts

Hubby's Pumpkin Pancakes

Missy Abbott
Hickory, PA

Give these pancakes a try...they are just scrumptious! My hubby created this recipe for me because I love flavored pancakes, but not all the sugar that's in them. I like mine lightly buttered with a drizzle of maple syrup. Simply delicious!

2 c. biscuit baking mix
1 egg, beaten
1-1/4 c. milk
1/2 c. canned pumpkin

1/3 c. walnuts, finely chopped
1-1/2 t. pumpkin pie spice
Garnish: favorite pancake
　　toppings

In a large bowl, combine all ingredients except garnish; stir together until well mixed. Add batter by 1/4 cupfuls onto a lightly oiled hot griddle. Cook until golden on both sides. Serve with your favorite toppings. Makes 8 pancakes.

Add a dash of whimsy to the breakfast table...
serve up maple syrup in Grandma's vintage
cow-shaped creamer.

Hillbilly Biscuits

Daniel Martin
Jacksonville, KY

These tasty biscuits are an easy breakfast idea that's perfect for family gatherings, potlucks or simply walking to the bus stop.

2 c. biscuit baking mix
2/3 c. buttermilk
3/4 c. shredded sharp Cheddar
   cheese

6-oz. pkg. real bacon bits
1 lb. ground pork breakfast
   sausage
1/4 c. butter, melted

In a bowl, combine biscuit mix, buttermilk, cheese, bacon bits and uncooked sausage. Mix with a spoon until well combined. Drop dough by heaping tablespoonfuls onto a parchment paper-lined baking sheet. Bake at 375 degrees for 15 to 20 minutes, until biscuits are golden and sausage is cooked. Remove from oven; immediately brush with melted butter. Serve warm. Makes 10 to 12 servings.

Caramel Apple Cinnamon Rolls

Marsha Baker
Pioneer, OH

This simple recipe is a terrific way to dress up canned rolls. Perfect for Christmas morning, or brunch any time of the year. Serve warm with coffee or milk...yum!

12.4-oz. tube refrigerated
   cinnamon rolls, separated
1 apple, cored and diced

Optional: chopped nuts
1 c. caramel sauce, divided

Arrange rolls in a sprayed 9" round baking pan; set aside frosting from tube. Sprinkle rolls evenly with apples and nuts, if desired; drizzle with half of caramel sauce. Bake at 375 degrees for 15 to 18 minutes, until golden. Cool slightly; drizzle with remaining caramel sauce and reserved frosting as desired. Serves 8.

Busy-Day Breakfast Shortcuts

Potato Tot Pizza

Rhonda Reeder
Ellicott City, MD

Easy to make and very tasty! Perfect for a late-night snack after the big game. A 9-inch round pan works well if you don't have a cast-iron skillet. Precooked bacon chopped with kitchen scissors saves time. Serve with catsup and hot pepper sauce.

30-oz. pkg. frozen potato
    puffs, thawed
1 to 2 T. butter
6 eggs, beaten
salt and pepper to taste

8-oz. pkg. shredded Cheddar
    cheese, divided
1/2 c. fully cooked bacon,
    chopped

Coat a cast-iron skillet with non-stick vegetable spray. Arrange potato puffs in the bottom and sides of skillet. Bake, uncovered, at 425 degrees for 15 minutes, or until golden. Meanwhile, melt butter in another skillet over medium-low heat; add eggs and scramble lightly. Season with salt and pepper. Remove skillet from oven; flatten potato puffs lightly with a spatula. Top with one cup of cheese, scrambled eggs and remaining cheese. Flatten again with spatula; top with crumbled bacon. Return to oven for 10 minutes, or until cheese is melted. Cool slightly; cut into wedges and serve. Makes 8 to 10 servings.

Butter-flavored non-stick vegetable spray is especially handy at breakfast time. Use it to spray skillets, pancake griddles and baking pans...done in a second, and clean-up is easy.

Orange Juice Muffins

Linda Crandall
Pulaski, NY

A perfect little pick-me-up at breakfast and snacktime.
You might already have the ingredients on hand!

2 c. biscuit baking mix
1 egg, beaten
1 t. orange zest
2/3 c. orange juice

4 T. sugar, divided
1/4 t. cinnamon
1/8 t. nutmeg

In a bowl, stir together biscuit mix, egg, orange zest, orange juice and 2 tablespoons sugar until moistened. Divide batter among 12 greased or paper-lined muffin cups, filling 2/3 full. Combine remaining sugar and spices in a cup; sprinkle evenly over muffins. Bake at 400 degrees for 15 minutes. Makes one dozen.

Most muffin batters can be stirred up the night before, and can even be scooped into muffin cups. Simply cover and refrigerate... in the morning, pop them in the oven. Your family will love waking up to the sweet smell of muffins baking!

Lemon Monkey Bread

Ann Farris
Biscoe, AR

This sweet-tart bread will melt in your mouth! It is so easy to make, which is a good thing, because it goes fast at our house.

12 frozen yeast dinner rolls, thawed but still cold
3 T. butter, melted
1/2 c. sugar

zest of 1 lemon
1/2 c. powdered sugar
1 T. lemon juice

Cut thawed rolls in half; arrange in a greased 13"x9" baking pan. Drizzle with melted butter; set aside. Mix together sugar and lemon zest in a cup; sprinkle half of mixture over rolls. Cover with a tea towel; let rise until double. Uncover; sprinkle with remaining sugar mixture. Bake at 350 degrees for 20 to 25 minutes. Remove from pan. In another bowl, stir together powdered sugar and lemon juice to a glaze consistency. Turn rolls out onto a plate; drizzle with glaze while still warm. Serves 6 to 10.

For a fruity cream cheese spread, combine 8 ounces of softened cream cheese and 1/4 cup peach preserves; mix until smooth. So delicious on warm slices of quick bread.

Crustless Broccoli Quiche

Vickie
Gooseberry Patch

This quiche is creamy and delicious...we love to share it on weekends. It's very versatile...chopped cooked asparagus, Gruyère cheese and crumbled bacon are yummy too. Extra slices can be kept in the fridge up to three days, for an easy meal another day.

4 eggs, beaten
1-2/3 c. milk
1 c. grated Parmesan cheese
3/4 c. biscuit baking mix
1/4 c. butter, softened
1 c. cooked ham, diced

10-oz. pkg. chopped frozen
broccoli, thawed and well
drained
8-oz. pkg. shredded Cheddar
cheese
salt and pepper to taste

In a large bowl, whisk together eggs, milk, Parmesan cheese, biscuit mix and butter until well combined; mixture will be lumpy. Fold in ham, broccoli and Cheddar cheese; season with salt and pepper. Spoon mixture into a lightly greased 10" quiche pan or pie plate. Bake, uncovered, at 375 degrees for 50 minutes, or until golden and eggs are set. Cut into wedges and serve. Makes 6 to 8 servings.

Bake a family-favorite quiche in muffin cups for individual servings in a jiffy. Reduce the baking time by about 10 minutes, and test for doneness with a toothpick.

Busy-Day Breakfast Shortcuts

Drew's Favorite Peaches & Cream Salad

Jessica Branch
Cholesterol, IL

This is a quick & easy salad I like to make for my daughter Drew, who just loves fresh fruit and fruit salad. It's scrumptious at breakfast... great for dessert too! When peaches are in season, use six ripe peaches, peeled, pitted and chopped.

32-oz. container vanilla yogurt
3-1/2 oz. pkg. instant vanilla
    pudding mix
8-oz. container frozen whipped
    topping, thawed

2 15-oz. cans sliced peaches,
    drained and chopped

In a large bowl, combine yogurt and dry pudding mix; stir until well blended. Fold in whipped topping and peaches. Cover and refrigerate before serving. Serves 10 to 12.

Keep early risers as well as sleepyheads happy with fresh, hot breakfasts...it's simple. Fill individual custard cups with a favorite baked oatmeal or breakfast casserole and pop into the oven as needed.

Granny's Garden Frittata

Jill Valentine
Jackson, TN

This wonderful dish reminds me of my grandmother going out to her garden to pick fresh vegetables for the meals she made for us. It's good just about any time of day...refrigerated potatoes make it a little quicker.

1 to 2 T. olive oil
20-oz. pkg. refrigerated diced
   potatoes with onions
1 c. zucchini, diced
1/2 c. red pepper, diced
1 t. seasoned salt, divided

1/4 t. garlic pepper
6 eggs, beaten
1/4 c. milk
1 to 1-1/2 c. shredded Cheddar
   cheese

Heat oil in a cast-iron skillet over medium-high heat. Add potatoes, zucchini, red pepper, 1/2 teaspoon salt and pepper. Cook and stir for 2 minutes. Reduce heat to low. Cover and cook for 8 to 10 minutes, stirring occasionally, until vegetables are tender. In a bowl, whisk together eggs, milk and remaining salt; pour over vegetables in skillet. Cover and cook over low heat for 10 minutes, or until eggs are nearly set. Place skillet under preheated broiler. Broil for 2 minutes, or until set and golden. Sprinkle with cheese; broil for one minute longer, just until cheese is melted. Cut into wedges and serve. Serves 4 to 6.

Breakfast for dinner is a fun and frugal treat. Enjoy waffles or French toast in the evening, when there's more time to cook. Add yummy fruit toppings and a side of sausage or bacon for a delicious complete meal.

Busy-Day Breakfast Shortcuts

Home-Fried Potatoes

Kathy Grashoff
Fort Wayne, IN

These tasty potatoes will be ready by the time you've finished cracking and scrambling your eggs.

2 T. butter
2 15-oz. cans sliced potatoes,
  well drained

1/2 t. garlic powder
1/2 t. onion powder
salt and pepper to taste

Melt butter in a skillet over medium heat; add potatoes. Stir gently until potatoes are well coated with butter. Sprinkle with seasonings. Cook and stir until heated through and golden. Makes 4 servings.

Lazy-Day Fruit Salad

Jessalyn Wantland
Napoleon, OH

An easy fruit salad that goes well with breakfast and lunch.

20-oz. can crushed pineapple
3.4-oz. pkg. instant vanilla
  pudding mix
8-oz. container frozen whipped
  topping, thawed

30-oz. can fruit cocktail, drained
15-oz. can mandarin oranges,
  drained

Pour pineapple with juice into a large bowl. Add dry pudding mix and stir well. Fold in whipped topping; stir in fruit cocktail and oranges. Serve immediately, or cover and chill. Serves 6 to 8.

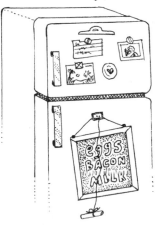

Keep shopping simple! On a chalkboard, list kitchen basics like milk, bread, cheese and eggs. Post the board on the fridge and check off items with chalk as they are used up.

German Streusel Coffee Cake

Judy Borecky
Escondido, CA

I recently found this recipe while going through some 1970s recipes from my mother-in-law, who passed away in 2008. I don't think it has ever been in print. Her parents were from Germany, and they settled in central Kansas and raised two children. Their last name was Mehl, which means "flour." I have recently made it twice and we really like it. It is so easy and you can have it made in no time.

18-1/2 oz. pkg. chocolate
   cake mix
3.4-oz. pkg. instant coconut
   pudding mix
4 eggs, beaten

1/2 c. oil
1 c. water
1/4 c. flaked coconut
1/4 c. chopped walnuts
1/2 c. semi-sweet chocolate chips

In a large bowl, combine cake mix, pudding mix, eggs, oil and water; beat well. Pour batter into a 12"x12" baking pan coated with non-stick vegetable spray. Sprinkle with coconut, walnuts and chocolate chips; top with Streusel. Bake at 350 degrees for 26 minutes, or until a toothpick tests done. Cut into squares. Makes 15 to 20 servings.

Streusel:

1/4 c. butter, melted
1/2 c. all-purpose flour

1/3 c. brown sugar, packed

Mix all ingredients well.

Perk up morning place settings in a wink...fill pint-size canning jars with cheery blooms.

Busy-Day Breakfast Shortcuts

Grandma's Easy Pancake & Sausage Stacks

Carolyn Deckard
Bedford, IN

Our family loved to have breakfast at Grandma's. She made her own homemade sausage to fry, and made her pancakes from scratch too. Now my family makes down-home breakfasts a lot easier by using frozen sausage patties and pancakes. We still have great memories of Grandma's each time we fix this recipe.

2 c. apples, cored and diced
1 c. maple-flavored syrup
1/2 t. cinnamon
8 frozen brown & serve pork
 sausage patties
8 frozen pancakes

In a saucepan over medium-high heat, combine apples, syrup and cinnamon. Bring to a boil; reduce heat to medium. Cook for about 5 minutes, stirring occasionally, until apples are tender. Meanwhile, separately heat sausage patties and pancakes as directed on packages. For each serving, stack one pancake, 2 sausage patties, a spoonful of apple mixture, one additional pancake and another spoonful of apple mixture. Serves 4.

Serve poached eggs with breakfast hash, atop a burger or a tossed salad. Fill a skillet with water and bring to a simmer. Swirl the water with a spoon and gently slide in an egg from a saucer. Let cook until set, about 2 minutes; remove egg with a slotted spoon.

Oh-So-Good French Toast

Becky Johnson
Spring, TX

So rich and delicious...well worth waking up for!

4 eggs, beaten
14-oz. can sweetened
   condensed milk
1 c. whole milk

1 T. vanilla extract
1 to 2 T. butter
8 slices frozen Texas toast
Garnish: butter, powdered sugar

In a large bowl, whisk together eggs, milks and vanilla; beat well and set aside. Melt butter in a skillet over medium heat. Dip toast into egg mixture, one slice at a time. Cook until lightly golden on both sides. Serve toast topped with butter and powdered sugar. Makes 8 servings.

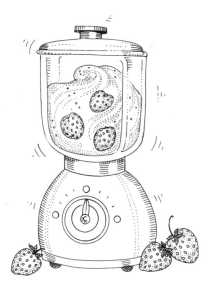

Whip up some scrumptious maple-berry syrup in a jiffy! Thaw 2 cups frozen strawberries or blueberries and add to a blender with 1/2 cup maple syrup. Process until smooth. Refrigerate up to 2 weeks.

Busy-Day Breakfast Shortcuts

Pecan Breakfast Rolls

Michelle Braggart
Castle Rock, CO

I've been making this recipe year after year, and my adult children still ask me ask if we are having the pecan rolls for Christmas morning! But, it's really too delicious to make just once a year.

1 to 2 T. butter, softened
1 c. chopped pecans
24 frozen yeast dinner rolls
3.4-oz. pkg. instant butterscotch
    pudding mix

1 c. brown sugar, packed
1/2 c. butter, melted

The night before, coat a 13"x9" baking pan with softened butter. Sprinkle chopped pecans evenly in pan; arrange frozen rolls in pan. Sprinkle rolls with dry pudding mix. Stir together brown sugar and melted butter; spoon over rolls. Cover with wax paper and place pan in cold oven overnight. The next day, remove pan from oven; preheat oven. Uncover pan and bake at 375 degrees for 20 to 25 minutes, until lightly golden. Remove from oven; flip pan over onto a parchment paper-lined baking sheet. Spoon any of the remaining mixture in pan over rolls and serve. Makes 2 dozen.

An oilcloth tablecloth with brightly colored fruit and flowers is so cheerful at breakfast...and sticky syrup and jam spills are easily wiped off with a damp sponge!

Simple Baked Eggs

Kerry Mayer
Dunham Springs, LA

No need to stand over a hot stove...these eggs will cook up fluffy
and tender in the oven while you're making buttered toast.
The more you whisk the eggs, the fluffier they'll be.

1 T. butter, softened
8 eggs, beaten
1-1/2 t. butter, melted
1/2 c. small-curd cottage cheese

2/3 c. shredded Cheddar cheese,
   divided
salt and pepper to taste

Generously coat an 8"x8" baking pan with softened butter; set aside. In
a large bowl, combine eggs, melted butter, cottage cheese and 1/3 cup
Cheddar cheese; whisk very well. Season with salt and pepper. Spoon
mixture into pan. Bake, uncovered, at 375 degrees for 20 minutes, or
until eggs are puffy and set, checking occasionally. Top with remaining
Cheddar cheese. Cut into squares and serve. Makes 6 servings.

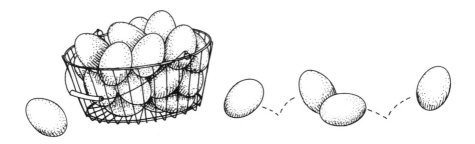

When breaking eggs, if part of a broken eggshell gets into
the bowl, just dip in half of an already-broken eggshell.
The broken bit will grab onto it like a magnet.

Busy-Day Breakfast Shortcuts

Sausage-Cream Cheese Breakfast Bake

Jessica Klaus
Delaware, OH

I have been making this casserole for Christmas morning for years. I always make two pans and they go fast! It's great for busy days and special days year 'round, too.

1 lb. ground pork breakfast
   sausage
8-oz. pkg. cream cheese, cubed
   and softened
1 doz. eggs, beaten

1/2 c. milk
2 8-oz. tubes refrigerated
   crescent rolls
8-oz. pkg. shredded Cheddar
   cheese

Brown sausage in a skillet over medium heat; drain. Add cream cheese; stir to combine and remove from heat. Meanwhile, in a large bowl, whisk together eggs and milk. Add to sausage mixture and stir well; set aside. Unroll one tube of crescent rolls in an ungreased 13"x9" baking pan; press down. Spread sausage mixture over rolls; top with shredded cheese. Top with remaining tube of crescent rolls. Bake, uncovered, at 375 degrees for 25 minutes. Serves 8 to 10.

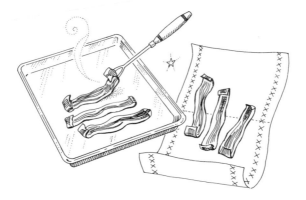

Crumbled bacon makes everything taste better! Here's an easy way to make it...even bake a pound at a time to freeze for future meals. Arrange bacon slices on a rimmed baking sheet and bake at 350 degrees. They'll be crisp in about 15 minutes, with no messy spatters!

Strawberry Cream Cheese Danish

Jill Burton
Gooseberry Patch

Ready in no time! I like to top these tender pastries with several different jams, so everyone can choose their favorite.

8-oz. tube refrigerated
   crescent rolls
1/3 c. cream cheese spread
1/2 c. plus 3 T. powdered
   sugar, divided

8 t. strawberry jam
1/4 c. sliced almonds
2 to 3 t. milk

Remove rolls from tube; do not unroll. With a serrated knife, cut dough into 8 slices. Arrange slices on an ungreased baking sheet, 2 inches apart. Flatten each slice into a 3-inch circle; form a rim around outer edge. In a small bowl, blend cream cheese spread and 3 tablespoons powdered sugar. Spoon 2 teaspoons of mixture into the center of each dough circle; spread slightly. Top each circle with one teaspoon jam; sprinkle with almonds. Bake at 375 degrees for 12 to 14 minutes, until golden. Cool on pan for 5 minutes; remove to a plate. In a small bowl, stir together remaining powdered sugar and milk to a drizzling consistency. Drizzle over pastries and serve warm. Makes 8 servings.

If it's a beautiful day, carry breakfast outdoors! Toss a colorful tablecloth on the picnic table and enjoy the fresh air and early-morning sunshine.

Busy-Day Breakfast Shortcuts

Quick & Easy Coffee Cake

Sandy Ward
Anderson, IN

*Love this easy fruit-filled coffee cake...it's great for
sharing with family & friends.*

3 eggs, beaten
15-1/4 oz. pkg. golden butter
  cake mix
20-oz. can favorite fruit
  pie filling

1 c. brown sugar, packed
2 T. butter, softened
2 T. all-purpose flour
1 c. chopped nuts
1 t. cinnamon

In a large bowl, beat together eggs and dry cake mix to make a
stiff batter. Stir in pie filling; spread batter in a greased and floured
13"x9" baking pan. In a separate bowl, mix together remaining
ingredients until crumbly; sprinkle over batter. Bake at 350 degrees
for 35 to 45 minutes. Cool slightly; cut into squares. Makes 12 to
15 servings.

With flavors like banana-nut, lemon poppy seed and even
birthday cake, muffin mix pancakes will never be boring!
To make, combine one 7-ounce muffin mix, 2/3 cup milk,
one egg and one tablespoon oil. Cook by 1/4 cupfuls on a
greased hot griddle and enjoy your pancakes!

Delicious Slow-Cooker Grits

Paula Marchesi
Auburn, PA

Yes, even a northerner can make incredible great-tasting grits. I get compliments all the time! Any type of shredded cheese will work, even horseradish cheese...mmm good. Serve for breakfast, or as a side for lunch or dinner.

2-2/3 c. water
1-1/2 c. milk
1-1/2 c. old-fashioned grits,
   uncooked
3 to 4 T. butter, cubed

2 t. chicken bouillon granules
1/2 t. salt
1 c. shredded white Cheddar
   cheese
1/3 c. grated Parmesan cheese

In a greased 3-quart slow cooker, combine water, milk, grits, butter, bouillon and salt; stir well. Cover and cook on low setting for 2-1/2 to 3 hours, stirring every 30 minutes, until liquid is absorbed and grits are tender. Stir in cheeses until melted. Serve immediately. Makes 6 servings.

Make breakfast fun for kids, especially on school days. Cut the centers from a slice of toast with a cookie cutter, serve milk or juice with twisty straws or put a smiley face on a bagel using raisins and cream cheese.

Busy-Day Breakfast Shortcuts

Scrambled Egg Muffins

Maureen Adamson
New Brunswick, Canada

This recipe has been popular at our morning gatherings after church service. Easy to make, easy to serve!

1/2 lb. ground pork sausage
1 doz. eggs, beaten
1/2 c. chopped onion
1/4 c. chopped green pepper
1/2 t. salt
1/4 t. pepper
1/2 c. shredded Cheddar cheese

Brown sausage in a skillet over medium heat; drain. Meanwhile, in a large bowl, stir together eggs, onion, green pepper, salt and pepper. Stir in sausage and cheese. Spoon mixture by 1/3 cupfuls into 12 greased muffin cups. Bake at 350 degrees for 20 to 25 minutes, until a knife tip inserted in the center comes out clean. Makes one dozen.

Sausage & Cheese Wraps

Elizabeth Smithson
Mayfield, KY

An old family favorite...I've been using this recipe for years. So easy to make and go. Try it with chopped ham, too!

16.3-oz. tube refrigerated
  jumbo biscuits
1/2 c. shredded Cheddar cheese
8 frozen brown & serve pork
  sausage links, sliced

Separate biscuits; press each biscuit flat. Evenly spoon cheese and sausage into the center of biscuits. Fold in half; press edges with a fork to seal. Arrange on an ungreased baking sheet. Bake at 375 degrees for 10 to 13 minutes, until golden. Makes 10 wraps.

For the fluffiest scrambled eggs ever, try Grandma's secret...stir in a pinch of baking powder!

Berry Fruity Smoothies

Elizabeth McCord
Memphis, TN

Smoothies are a favorite breakfast or snack. One of my favorite things is coming up with new flavor combinations. This one is so bright and fresh!

2/3 c. milk
2/3 c. orange juice
1/3 c. plain yogurt or vanilla
  ice cream

2 c. frozen mixed fruit
1/4 c. quick-cooking oats,
  uncooked
4 ice cubes

Combine all ingredients in a blender. Process very well until smooth. Pour into 2 glasses and serve. Makes 2 servings.

Out-the-Door Delight

Amy Thomason Hunt
Traphill, NC

Quick, easy, nutritious and delicious! Use your favorite fruit and yogurt...swap out the bran cereal for granola.

2 c. canned diced peaches in
  light syrup, drained
16-oz. container low-fat
  peach yogurt

2 c. bran & raisin cereal

Layer peaches and yogurt evenly among 4, 16-ounce plastic cups. Top with cereal. Serve immediately, or cover and refrigerate. Makes 4 servings.

There is no doubt that running
away on a fresh blue morning
can be exhilarating.

–Jean Rhys

Snacks & Sandwiches to Share

Ham & Cheese Roll-Ups

*Shirley Howie
Foxboro, MA*

With only three ingredients, these roll-ups are a cinch to make! Sometimes I assemble the roll in the morning and just pop it into the oven at lunchtime. It couldn't be easier, and tastes really yummy served with a cup of tomato soup.

13.8-oz. tube refrigerated
   pizza dough
1/2 lb. deli baked ham,
   thinly sliced

1 c. shredded mozzarella cheese
Optional: mustard, horseradish
   sauce

Roll out pizza dough onto a lightly floured surface; press to form a 12-inch by 8-inch rectangle. Arrange ham slices evenly over dough to within 1/2 inch of edges. Sprinkle evenly with cheese. Starting at one short end, roll up dough to form a log. Pinch seams together to seal; place log seam-side down on a greased baking sheet. Bake at 400 degrees for 25 to 30 minutes, until deeply golden. Let stand for 10 minutes; cut into 8 slices with a serrated knife. Serve warm, with mustard or horseradish sauce, if desired. Serves 4.

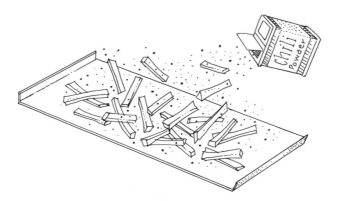

For zesty French fries, spray frozen fries with non-stick olive oil spray and sprinkle with your favorite spice blend. Spread on a baking sheet and bake as directed.

Philly Cheese Steak Wraps

*Karen Wilson
Defiance, OH*

*This delicious variation of Philly cheese steak sandwiches
is made with tortillas. It's ready in just minutes!*

2 c. frozen sweet pepper
   stir-fry mix
1/2 lb. deli roast beef,
   thinly sliced

1/4 c. Italian salad dressing
4 7-inch flour tortillas
1 c. shredded Monterey
   Jack cheese

In a non-stick skillet, cook and stir frozen pepper mix over medium-high
heat for 3 to 5 minutes, until tender. Stir in beef and salad dressing;
cook until heated through. Spoon 1/4 of beef mixture down the center
of each tortilla. Top each with 1/4 cup shredded cheese. Roll up tortillas
and serve warm. Makes 4 servings.

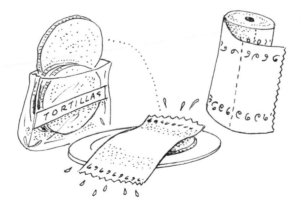

Warm up tortillas for your favorite recipe. Place several tortillas
on a microwave-safe plate and cover with a dampened
paper towel. Microwave on high for 30 seconds to one minute.

Easy Creamed Chicken Sandwiches

Marsha Baker
Pioneer, OH

This is a popular recipe here in Ohio, where it is often enjoyed at potlucks, ball games and graduation open houses. It is always a hit, and it couldn't be simpler.

2 13-oz. cans chicken breast
1 c. chicken broth
2 t. dried, flaked onions
1 t. chicken soup base
pepper to taste

10 to 12 saltines or buttery
   round crackers, crushed
6 to 8 soft sandwich buns, split
   and warmed

Add chicken with liquid to a large saucepan; break up with a fork. Add enough chicken broth to cover chicken. Stir in onions, soup base and pepper; add crushed crackers and stir. Simmer over low heat until heated through. Mixture will thicken up as it sets. May be transferred to a slow cooker to keep warm. Serve on warmed buns. Makes 6 to 8 servings.

Mini slider bun versions of favorite sandwiches are so appealing! Diners with light appetites can take just one, while those with heartier tastes can sample 2 or 3. Look for buns in tasty flavors like rye, pretzel and Hawaiian as well as soft white. Dinner rolls work well too.

Snacks & Sandwiches to Share

Bacon & Tomato Dip

Roberta Simpkins
Mentor on the Lake, OH

Serve this yummy dip on toasted baguette or with crackers. I have also filled lettuce leaves with this dip and served as lettuce rolls...it's like a mock BLT!

6 slices fully cooked bacon, chopped, or 1/2 c. real bacon bits
8-oz. pkg. cream cheese, cubed and softened

1/4 c. light or regular mayonnaise
2 T. fresh basil, chopped
1 ripe tomato, chopped
1/8 t. pepper

Warm bacon according to package directions. Crumble bacon into a food processor. Add remaining ingredients; pulse until smooth, using steel blade attachment. Transfer to a bowl; cover and chill until serving time. Makes 12 servings.

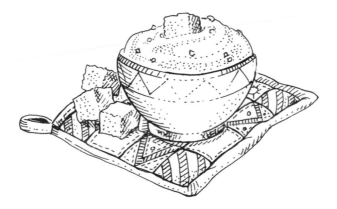

Baguette chips in a hurry! Pick up a bag of ready-sliced baguette at the deli. Arrange slices on a baking sheet, drizzle with olive oil and bake at 350 degrees for 10 minutes, or until crisp and golden.

Pepperoni Bread

Donna Parks
Jacksonville, TX

Every holiday, someone will ask for this appetizer. It's wonderful right out of the oven. I first had this in college, but made with sausage instead of pepperoni. I reworked it for my taste.

1 T. oil
1 frozen loaf bread dough
California garlic salt to taste
1/2 to 1 lb. sliced pepperoni

1/2 to 1 lb. sliced mozzarella
   cheese
1 egg, beaten
1 t. water

Spread oil in a large bowl; add frozen loaf. Cover with plastic wrap; allow to thaw overnight, or until thawed and dough is overflowing bowl. Remove dough to a floured surface. Knead and flatten with both hands into a square, about 12 inches by 8 inches. Sprinkle dough with garlic salt. Arrange pepperoni slices on top; layer with cheese, arranging all the slices in the same direction. Roll up loaf, starting on one long edge. Whisk together egg and water; brush some of egg mixture on edges to seal. Fold in sides. Place loaf on a large lightly greased baking sheet. Brush the top with remaining egg; sprinkle with more garlic salt. Bake at 350 degrees for one hour, or until golden. Slice and serve immediately. May also cool completely, wrap in aluminum foil and refrigerate; heat in microwave to serve. Makes one loaf; serves 6 to 8.

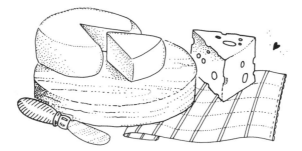

Check out artisan cheese selections at the deli counter for new varieties like Horseradish Cheddar and Habanero Gouda that will really add new flavor to favorite sandwiches.

Snacks & Sandwiches to Share

Million-Dollar Dip

Ann Farris
Biscoe, AR

This is my go-to appetizer when I need something quick...I always have the ingredients on hand. Serve with crackers.

8-oz. pkg. cream cheese, softened
8-oz. pkg. shredded Cheddar cheese
1/2 c. sour cream

8 slices fully cooked bacon, warmed and chopped
1/2 c. slivered almonds
1/4 c. green onions, diced

Combine all ingredients in a large bowl; blend well. Cover and chill for at least 2 hours. Makes 12 servings.

Hot Artichoke Dip

Julie Perkins
Anderson, IN

Simple to make...simply delicious to eat! Serve with snack crackers or white tortilla chips.

12-oz. pkg. shredded Parmesan cheese
3/4 c. mayonnaise

14-oz. can artichoke hearts, drained
1 t. pepper

Combine all ingredients in a bowl; mix well. Spoon into a lightly greased one-quart casserole dish. Bake, uncovered, at 350 degrees for 30 minutes, until hot and bubbly. Serves 6 to 8.

A quick and tasty appetizer in an instant! Place a block of cream cheese on a serving plate, spoon sweet-hot pepper jelly over it and serve with crisp crackers. Works great with spicy salsa or fruit chutney, too.

Pulled Pork Sandwiches

Kristin Gresham
Hobbs, NM

Easy quick prep! Have a tasty meal waiting for your family when they get home. I use the full 1/2 cup of cider vinegar, we love the tang. You can adjust it to your family's taste.

10-3/4 oz. can cream of
  onion soup
1/2 c. catsup
1/4 to 1/2 c. cider vinegar

3 to 4-lb. pork shoulder roast
8 to 10 hamburger buns or
  rolls, split

Mix onion soup, catsup and vinegar in a 4-quart slow cooker. Add pork; turn to coat with soup mixture. Cover and cook on low setting for 8 hours, or on high setting for 4 hours, until pork is very tender. Shred pork with 2 forks; serve on buns or rolls. Makes 8 to 10 servings.

A rainy-day cure-all...toss together ingredients for a tasty slow-cooker meal, pop some popcorn and enjoy a family movie marathon. When you're ready for supper, it's ready for you!

Snacks & Sandwiches to Share

Garlic Ranch Pretzels

Marsha Baker
Pioneer, OH

No baking needed! I've been making this scrumptious make-ahead snack for many years and am often asked to share the recipe. I've even had a four-year-old boy ask me how they are made...he loved them so much!

2 16-oz. pkgs. mini
   pretzel twists
12-oz. bottle butter-flavored
   popping oil

1-oz. pkg. ranch salad
   dressing mix
Optional: 2 to 3 t. garlic powder

Add pretzels to a 2-gallon plastic zipping bag; set bag in a pan on the counter. Drizzle with oil; shake bag to cover pretzels evenly with oil. Sprinkle with salad dressing mix; shake again until mixed well. Sprinkle garlic powder over pretzels, if using. Seal bag. Let stand for 8 hours or overnight, stirring or shaking bag every 2 hours or so. Transfer pretzels to a sealed container; will keep well for several weeks. Makes 20 servings.

Save the plastic liners when you toss out empty cereal boxes. They're perfect for storing homemade crispy treats and snack mixes.

Pineapple Barbecued Meatballs

Zoe Bennett
Columbia, SC

Serve with ruffled toothpicks for a wonderful party treat.

40-oz. pkg. frozen cooked
  meatballs
20-oz. can pineapple chunks,
  drained

2 16-oz. bottles barbecue sauce
16-oz. jar apricot preserves
1/2 c. brown sugar, packed

Add frozen meatballs to a large, deep skillet; stir in remaining ingredients. Simmer over low heat for about 20 minutes, stirring occasionally, until meatballs are glazed and cooked through. Serves 8 to 12.

Easy Ham Spread

Beckie Apple
Grannis, AR

This easy spread is one of my favorite quick cracker or sandwich spreads...it's a very tasty appetizer! Serve with assorted crackers, or use it to make sandwiches cut into triangles.

2 5-oz. cans chunk ham
3 T. mayonnaise
1 T. spicy brown mustard
1 t. dried, minced onions

1 t. hot pepper sauce
1/4 t. garlic powder
1/8 t. coarse pepper

In a bowl, use a fork to mash ham finely. Add remaining ingredients and stir well. Cover and chill until serving time. Makes 4 to 6 servings.

Set out all the fixin's for mini pizzas... flatbreads or English muffins, squeezable pizza sauce and cheese. Let the kids add their favorite toppers, then pop the pizzas in the oven at 375 degrees, until golden. A great little treat anytime!

Snacks & Sandwiches to Share

Reuben Roll-Ups

Karen Wilson
Defiance, OH

If you like Reuben sandwiches, you're going to love these quick & easy appetizers.

8-oz. tube refrigerated
   crescent rolls
8-oz. can sauerkraut, well
   drained
1/2 c. Thousand Island
   salad dressing

8 thin slices deli corned beef
2 slices Swiss cheese, cut into
   1/2-inch strips

Separate crescent rolls into 8 triangles; set aside. Add sauerkraut to a bowl; snip drained sauerkraut to cut long strands. Add salad dressing and mix well. To assemble, place one slice corned beef across the wide end of each triangle. Spread 2 tablespoons sauerkraut mixture on corned beef; top with 2 strips Swiss cheese. Roll up, beginning at the wide end. Place on a parchment paper-lined baking sheet. Bake at 375 degrees for 12 to 15 minutes. Serve warm. Serves 4 to 8.

If you want to feel rich, just count all of the things you have that money can't buy.
– Unknown

Potato Patch Pizza

Amy Thomason Hunt
Traphill, NC

*This recipe arrived tucked into my monthly phone bill. I gave it a try and thought it would be a good recipe for a **Gooseberry Patch** cookbook. It's quick & easy for busy nights or get-togethers.*

10-oz. tube refrigerated pizza
    crust dough
2 c. mashed potatoes
8-oz. pkg. shredded Cheddar
    cheese, divided

3-oz. jar real bacon bits
8 green onions, chopped
Garnish: sour cream

Cut pizza dough in half; spread in the bottom of 2, 9" round cake pans. Bake at 425 degrees for 4 minutes. Meanwhile, in a large bowl, combine potatoes, one cup cheese, bacon bits and onions. Spoon potato mixture evenly over each crust; sprinkle with remaining cheese. Bake an additional 5 minutes, or until cheese is melted and crusts are golden. Let cool; top with sour cream. Cut into wedges and serve. Makes 2 pizzas; each serves 6 to 8.

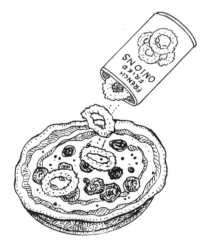

Add a crispy flavor punch to any dish with French fried onions. Try them sprinkled on pizza...heap them on burgers and deli sandwiches. Yum!

Snacks & Sandwiches to Share

Italian Sloppy Joes

Therese Scheckel
North Aurora, IL

I don't remember exactly how I got this recipe, but my family has been enjoying for years! You can use any amount of equal parts ground beef and Italian sausage. Add a little more pizza sauce, if you like it a little juicier.

1 lb. ground beef chuck
1 lb. Italian ground mild or
    hot pork sausage
12-oz. can pizza sauce

8-oz. pkg. shredded mozzarella
    cheese
6 to 8 Italian buns, split and
    hollowed out

In a large skillet over medium heat, brown beef and sausage together, crumbling well; drain. Stir in pizza sauce; simmer over low heat for about 10 minutes. Stir in cheese and cover until cheese melts. Stir well; spoon into hollowed-out buns. Makes 6 to 8 servings.

Encourage the kids try some new veggies! Try tempting them with fresh baby-size vegetables and a favorite ready-to-serve dip like hummus, ranch dressing or peanut butter. Great for snacking or as a side dish.

Freezer-Friendly Biscuit Sandwiches

Shari Rogers
San Leandro, CA

I like to make several batches of these for the freezer, so I can just grab one and microwave it as needed.

16.3-oz. tube refrigerated
   jumbo biscuits
8 slices deli ham, salami, turkey
   or roast beef

8 slices cheese, any variety

Bake biscuits as directed on package; let cool completely on a wire rack. Split biscuits. Place one slice of deli meat on each biscuit half, folding it to fit, if necessary. Cut each slice of cheese in half; place cheese halves on top of meat in an X. Replace tops of biscuits. Label and date a gallon-size plastic freezer bag. Place each sandwich into an individual plastic sandwich bag; place sandwiches in freezer bag. Freeze up to 3 months. To reheat, unwrap one sandwich; place on a microwave-safe plate. Microwave for 30 seconds, or until heated through. Serve warm. Makes 8 servings.

Wrapping up stacks of sandwiches? With a pop-up box of ready-cut aluminum foil squares, you'll have the job done in a jiffy!

Cheesy Pizzeria Bread Sticks

Cindy Neel
Gooseberry Patch

These are so easy to make...great with soup or pasta meals. Sometimes I'll use shredded Italian-blend cheese, or simply give it a sprinkle of Italian seasoning.

1 frozen loaf bread dough, thawed but still chilled
1/4 c. butter, melted

2 t. garlic, minced
8-oz. pkg. shredded mozzarella cheese

Spray counter with non-stick vegetable spray; roll out loaf into a 13-inch by 8-inch rectangle. Transfer dough to a sprayed baking sheet. Cover with sprayed plastic wrap; let rise for 45 minutes to one hour. Combine melted butter and garlic; stir to combine. Remove plastic wrap from dough; brush with butter mixture. Sprinkle evenly with cheese. Bake at 350 degrees for 20 minutes, or until cheese is melted and lightly golden. Cut into sticks and serve. Makes one dozen.

Just for fun, have appetizers for dinner! Set up a family-size sampler with mozzarella sticks, mini pizza snacks, mini egg rolls, potato skins and a bunch of dippers to try too.

Ranch Egg Salad Croissant Sandwiches

Carolyn Deckard
Bedford, IN

One of my husband's favorites! Can't remember where I got this great egg salad recipe. We love to have this for an easy brunch or lunch on busy days.

9 eggs, hard-boiled, peeled
   and halved
1/4 c. green onions, chopped
1/4 t. salt

1/4 t. pepper
1/2 c. ranch salad dressing
6 croissants, split
3 c. lettuce, shredded

Remove egg yolks to a large bowl; place egg whites in another bowl and set aside. Mash yolks with a fork; stir in onions, salt, pepper and salad dressing. Chop egg whites; stir into yolk mixture. For each sandwich, top the bottom half of one croissant with 1/2 cup lettuce and 1/2 cup egg mixture. Cover with top half of croissant and serve. Makes 6 servings.

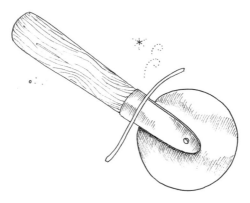

Use a pizza cutter to chop a bowlful of hard-cooked eggs in a jiffy! Just roll the cutter back & forth until eggs are chopped.

Snacks & Sandwiches to Share

Chili-Cheese Crescent Dogs

Ann Farris
Biscoe, AR

These are so easy! I usually keep the ingredients on hand, so I can make a quick meal anytime in less than 20 minutes..

8-oz. tube refrigerated
   crescent rolls
8 hot dogs
1 c. shredded Colby Jack or
   Cheddar cheese, divided

15-oz. can hot dog chili sauce
Optional: diced onions, sliced
   jalapeño peppers

Unroll crescent dough; separate triangles. Place each hot dog on the wide end of a triangle. Sprinkle with a little shredded cheese and roll up. Arrange in a lightly greased 13"x9" baking pan. Bake, uncovered, at 375 degrees for 8 to 10 minutes, just until crescents are beginning to turn golden. Remove from oven; top with chili sauce and remaining cheese. Return to oven for another 3 to 5 minutes, until cheese melts and crescents are golden. Top with onions and/or jalapeño, if desired. Makes 8 servings.

Pizza Burgers

Georgie Waybright
Beverly, WV

I am a grandmother and I love to garden. Quilting and going camping at my cabin are my pastimes. My kids just love these open-face burgers and want them every day while watching cartoons! They're very good and easy to make.

4 hamburger buns, split
1 lb. ground beef
10-3/4 oz. can tomato soup

1/2 t. Italian seasoning
8 slices American cheese

Arrange buns on a baking sheet, cut-side up. Bake at 350 degrees for 5 minutes, or until lightly toasted; set aside. Meanwhile, in a skillet over medium heat, brown beef well; drain. Stir in soup and seasoning; heat through. Spoon beef mixture over buns on baking sheet; add a cheese slice to each. Return to oven for a few minutes, until cheese melts. Makes 8 servings.

Spicy Pecan Pimento Cheese

Martha Stapler
Sanford, FL

A great appetizer with crackers...this spread makes
a killer grilled cheese sandwich, too!

8-oz. pkg. cream cheese,
　softened
8-oz. pkg. shredded taco-blend
　cheese
1/2 c. mayonnaise

1/4 t. to 1/2 t. cayenne pepper,
　to taste
4-oz. jar diced pimentos, drained
3/4 c. chopped pecans

Combine cheeses and mayonnaise in a large bowl. Beat with an electric mixer on medium speed until blended. Add remaining ingredients; beat on low speed until blended. Cover and chill until serving time. Makes 9 servings.

Tasty homemade crackers...simple! Roll out refrigerated pie crusts into a 12-inch round. Drizzle lightly with olive oil and sprinkle with salt. Use a pizza cutter to cut crusts into small squares. Bake on a parchment paper-lined baking sheet at 450 degrees for 6 to 7 minutes, until crisp.

Snacks & Sandwiches to Share

Easy Cheeseburger Pizza

Judy Lange
Imperial, PA

If you like cheeseburgers, you will love this pizza...yum!

10-oz. tube refrigerated
   pizza crust
1/2 lb. extra-lean ground beef
1 c. spaghetti sauce

1/4 c. red onion, chopped
1 c. shredded Cheddar cheese
1/4 c. dill pickle slices, drained

Unroll dough and place in a 12" round pizza pan coated with non-stick vegetable spray. Starting at the center, press out dough with your hands to form a 1/2-inch rim. Bake at 425 degrees for 7 to 9 minutes; set aside. Meanwhile, brown beef in a skillet over medium heat; drain. Spread spaghetti sauce evenly over baked crust; top with beef, onion and cheese. Return to oven and bake an additional 12 to 18 minutes, until bubbly and edges are golden. Cut into wedges; top with pickle slices and serve. Makes 4 servings.

Save that jar of dill pickle juice after the pickles are gone. Add peeled, warm hard-boiled eggs to the juice, cover and refrigerate for a few days. The eggs will absorb the dilly juice...a great addition to your relish tray! Try it with bread-and-butter pickle juice too.

Speedy Vegetarian Bean Dip

Caroline Miller
Stonington, CT

My family loves this bean dip! It's very versatile and comes together in minutes. You can add additional ingredients like green chiles, diced tomatoes or corn to suite your family's tastes. This dip can also be part of a seven-layer dip, enjoyed inside tacos or burritos or simply served with rice. Yum!

16-oz. can refried beans
8-oz. pkg. pasteurized process
    cheese, cubed

2 T. taco seasoning mix
Garnish: sour cream

In a large saucepan, combine refried beans and cheese cubes. Cook and stir over medium heat until cheese melts. Stir in taco seasoning until mixed well. Transfer to a bowl; top with sour cream and serve. Makes 8 servings.

Sweet Onion Spread

Irene Robinson
Cincinnati, OH

Super-simple to make, with only three ingredients. Serve with snack crackers, bread sticks or party rye bread.

1 c. sweet onion, finely chopped
1 c. mayonnaise

1 c. shredded Swiss or
    Cheddar cheese

Mix together all ingredients in a large bowl; spread in a lightly greased one-quart casserole dish. Bake, uncovered, at 350 degrees for 20 to 30 minutes, until bubbly and golden. Serves 8 to 10.

For the easiest-ever snacking mix, toss together equal amounts of sweetened dried cranberries, salted peanuts and chocolate chips.

Snacks & Sandwiches to Share

Basil-Vegetable Cheese Spread

Doreen Knapp
Stanfordville, NY

This spread was always served at our house for Christmas and Thanksgiving. Serve with rustic crackers or crusty bread.

2 8-oz. pkgs. cream cheese, softened
1/2 c. butter, softened
1/4 c. fresh basil, chopped, or 2 T. dried basil
2 T. shredded Parmesan cheese
1/2 c. chopped almonds
1.4-oz. pkg. vegetable soup mix

In a large bowl, beat cream cheese with an electric mixer on medium speed until soft. Add butter; beat until blended and smooth. Add remaining ingredients and beat well until combined. Line an 8-1/2"x4-1/2" loaf pan with parchment paper. Spoon cream cheese mixture into pan, pushing down into pan. Cover and refrigerate for 2 to 4 hours. Turn out onto a serving platter; remove parchment paper and serve. Makes 6 servings.

Roasted artichokes are tasty and easy. Drain two 14-ounce cans of artichoke hearts. Cut in half and pat very dry. Spread a rimmed baking sheet with one tablespoon olive oil. Arrange artichokes on pan, cut-side down. Bake on the bottom oven rack at 425 degrees for 10 to 12 minutes, until golden. Sprinkle with lemon zest, thyme and a little salt and pepper; toss to combine and enjoy warm.

Pantry Clean-Out Snack Mix

Shelby Brookings
West Hills, CA

I make this snack mix any time I have extra boxes or half-used boxes of snacks and cereals in the pantry. You can add just about anything and still create a tasty snack!

14-oz. pkg. bite-size crispy rice cereal squares
14-oz. pkg. bite-size crispy corn cereal squares
1/2 to 1 c. doughnut-shaped honey-nut oat cereal
1/2 to 1 c. mini cookies, crackers or pretzel twists
1/2 to 1 c. pumpkin or sunflower seeds
1/2 to 1 c. peanuts, pecans, cashews, hazelnuts or Brazil nuts
1 c. butter, melted
1/4 c. Worcestershire sauce or soy sauce
1 T. onion powder
1 T. seasoned salt

In a huge bowl, combine all cereals, crackers, cookies, seeds and nuts. Drizzle with melted butter and Worcestershire or soy sauce; sprinkle with seasonings. Toss to mix well. Divide mixture evenly between 2 ungreased large rimmed baking sheets. Bake at 375 degrees for 12 to 15 minutes, until all ingredients are golden and lightly toasted. Let cool and serve; or store in an airtight container. Makes 20 servings.

When you're putting away groceries, be sure to label any ingredients that are intended for dinner...that way, Wednesday's supper won't turn into Tuesday's after-school snack! Set aside cheese cubes, veggies and fruit labeled "OK for snacking" to tame appetites.

Snacks & Sandwiches to Share

French Dip Sandwiches

Karen Chandler
Madison Heights, MI

These are my daughter's favorite sandwiches. She will not eat French dip sandwiches in a restaurant...she says they are never as good as these! If you prefer, use six French sub rolls instead of the loaf, and wrap each individually with aluminum foil.

14-oz. can beef broth
1-oz. env. onion soup mix
1-1/2 lb. beef chuck roast

16-oz. loaf French bread
1-1/2 c. shredded mozzarella
   cheese

Stir together beef broth and soup mix in a 4-quart slow cooker; add roast and turn to coat. Cover and cook on low setting for 7 to 8 hours, until roast is very tender. Remove roast from slow cooker, reserving broth; skim fat from broth as desired. Shred roast with 2 forks and set aside. Slice bread loaf lengthwise, but do not cut through. Stuff loaf with beef and cheese; wrap entire loaf in aluminum foil. Bake at 350 degrees for 15 to 20 minutes, until hot and cheese melts. Slice loaf into 6 servings. Serve sandwiches with reserved broth for dipping. Makes 6 servings.

Pick up a stack of vintage plastic burger baskets. Lined with crisp paper napkins, they're fun for serving sandwiches, chips and a pickle spear. Clean-up after dinner is a snap too!

Chicken-Stuffed French Bread

Joan Raven
Cicero, NY

I have been making this recipe for family & friends for years.
Easy-peasy and oh-so delicious...get ready for ooohs and ahhhhs!

1 loaf French bread, halved
   lengthwise
1 lb. boneless, skinless chicken
   breasts, cooked and shredded
1-1/2 c. shredded Colby Jack
   cheese

3 green onions, thinly sliced
1 to 2 c. ranch salad dressing
cracked pepper to taste

Arrange halves of loaf on a parchment paper-lined baking sheet; cut-side up; set aside. In a large bowl, combine chicken, cheese, green onions and enough salad dressing to moisten mixture. Mix well; season with pepper. Spread chicken mixture evenly over half of loaf; top with other half. Bake at 375 degrees for 10 to 15 minutes, until heated through and cheese is melted. Remove from oven; let stand 5 minutes. Slice and serve. Serves 4 to 6.

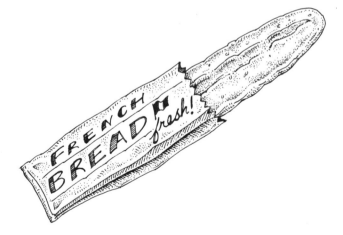

Mayo and mustard are good ol' sandwich partners...
check the fridge for other spreads, too! Add lively new
flavor to sandwiches with pesto sauce, hummus,
fruit preserves or pepper jelly.

Snacks & Sandwiches to Share

Hot Cheddar Corn Dip

JoAnn
Gooseberry Patch

Need a quick snack? This delicious hot dip goes together in no time. Serve with your favorite tortilla chips.

1/2 c. cream cheese, softened
3/4 c. spicy chipotle ranch salad
  dressing

1 c. frozen corn, thawed
1 c. shredded Mexican-blend
  cheese, divided

Combine cream cheese, salad dressing, corn and 1/2 cup shredded cheese in a large bowl. Beat with an electric mixer on medium speed until well blended. Transfer to a greased 2-cup casserole dish; top with remaining cheese. Bake, uncovered, at 375 degrees for about 10 minutes, until hot and bubbly. Makes 1-1/2 cups.

Cool Broccomole Dip

Teresa Verell
Roanoke, VA

This tasty recipe is always served on our family movie night. It's very similar to guacamole dip. Serve with buttery round crackers and tortilla chips.

2 c. frozen chopped broccoli,
  cooked and cooled
2 T. mayonnaise
1/4 c. sour cream

1 T. sweet onion, minced
1 t. lemon juice
1 t. lime juice
1/8 t. chili powder

Combine all ingredients in a food processor; process until smooth. Transfer to a bowl; cover and refrigerate for 6 hours. Serves 5.

For a quick last-minute party appetizer, drain a jar of Italian antipasto mix and toss with bite-size cubes of provolone cheese. Serve with cocktail picks.

Cheesy Chicken Dip

Sherry Lamb Noble
Paragould, AR

This dip is so good, you'll want to double the recipe! You can substitute a cheese of your choice for the Parmesan cheese.

8-oz. pkg. cream cheese,
   softened
8-oz. container sour cream
12-1/2 oz. can chunk chicken
   breast, drained

1/2 c. onion, diced
1/8 t. garlic salt
1 to 1-1/2 c. shredded Parmesan
   cheese

In a large bowl, mix together all ingredients except Parmesan cheese. Spoon into a lightly greased one-quart casserole dish; top with cheese. Bake, uncovered, at 350 degrees for 30 to 40 minutes, until bubbly and cheese is golden. Makes 8 servings.

Snack packs in a flash! Fill mini plastic zipping bags with individual portions of goldfish crackers, trail mix or mini pretzels. Gather all the little bags into one big container...all ready for treats as they're needed.

Snacks & Sandwiches to Share

Hot Crab Dip

Gladys Kielar
Whitehouse, OH

Serve this tasty dip right from the slow cooker, with crackers and chunks of bread for dipping. It's a party in a crock!

1/2 c. milk
1/3 c. favorite salsa
3 8-oz. pkgs. cream cheese, cubed and softened
2 8-oz. pkgs. imitation crabmeat, flaked

1 c. green onions, thinly sliced
4-oz. can chopped green chiles, drained

Combine milk and salsa in a lightly greased 3-quart slow cooker. Stir in remaining ingredients. Cover and cook on low setting for 3 to 4 hours, stirring every 30 minutes, until hot and bubbly. Makes 10 servings.

Cream Cheese Shrimp Dip

Sheri Haney
Winchester, IN

This dip is so simple to do...it goes together in a snap! My family will make a meal of this dip along with some veggies and dip, pickles, olives and other finger foods.

8-oz. pkg. cream cheese, room temperature
1 to 2 4-oz. cans tiny shrimp, well drained

12-oz. bottle cocktail sauce
2 to 3 sleeves buttery round crackers

Unwrap cream cheese and place on a large serving plate. Spoon shrimp over cheese; some may fall off to the side, but just scoop them onto the cheese. Spoon cocktail sauce over shrimp. Serve with crackers. Makes 6 servings.

Keep the pantry tidy...tuck packets of seasoning mix into a napkin holder.

Tangy Barbecue Ham Sandwiches

Tammy Navarro
Littleton, CO

These saucy, tangy sandwiches can be on your table in no time! I like to serve them with baked beans and homemade mac & cheese.

1/2 c. catsup
1/2 c. water
1 T. brown sugar, packed
1-1/2 t. Worcestershire sauce

1-1/2 t. vinegar
3/4 t. cinnamon
1 lb. deli chipped ham
8 hamburger buns, split

In a large saucepan, combine all ingredients except ham and buns. Bring to a boil over medium heat; reduce heat to medium-low. Simmer for 10 to 15 minutes, stirring occasionally. Stir in ham and simmer another 10 minutes. To serve, spoon ham mixture onto buns. Makes 8 servings.

Toast sandwich buns in a buttered skillet before adding shredded or sliced meat. It only takes a minute and makes such a tasty difference. Buns will drip less, too.

Snacks & Sandwiches to Share

Favorite Hot Spinach Dip

Caroline Britt
Cleveland, TX

This recipe is simple, yet very flavorful. We love spinach dip, but it can be quite expensive, bought ready-made. That's why we created this recipe! It's great with tortilla chips or sturdy crackers.

16-oz. pkg. frozen chopped
  spinach
2 8-oz. pkgs. cream cheese,
  softened and cubed

14-1/2 oz. can diced tomatoes
  with green chiles, drained
8-oz. pkg. shredded Italian-blend
  cheese, divided

In a large saucepan, cook spinach according to package directions; drain well. Add cream cheese, tomatoes and 1/2 cup shredded cheese; mix well. Spoon into a lightly greased 2-quart casserole dish. Bake, uncovered, at 350 degrees for 30 minutes. Top with remaining cheese and bake for a few more minutes, until cheese is melted. Makes 24 servings.

Vicki's Horseradish Dip

Patricia Shears Jones
Stillwater, NJ

I received this recipe many years ago from my sister-in-law Vicki. It's just a simple dip that everyone loves, but no one can ever guess the main ingredient! Serve with mini pretzels.

8-oz. pkg. cream cheese,
  softened
2 to 3 T. prepared horseradish,
  to taste

2 to 3 T. sugar, to taste

Mix together all ingredients in a bowl. Cover and chill until serving time. Makes 6 to 8 servings.

Freeze giant ice cubes in muffin tins for a party pitcher of lemonade...they'll last much longer than regular ice cubes.

Shrimp Poor Boys

Lorna Dressler
Universal City, TX

*We lived in Biloxi, Mississippi for two years and fell in love with
poor boy sandwiches. Now that we are living in Texas,
I can recreate them and bring back fond memories.*

24 frozen breaded shrimp
4 French bread rolls or hot dog
   buns, split

tartar sauce to taste
1-1/2 c. lettuce, shredded
Optional: chopped tomatoes

Bake shrimp according to package directions. Meanwhile, toast rolls and
spread with tartar sauce. To serve, top each roll with 6 shrimp. Sprinkle
with lettuce and tomatoes, if desired; serve. Makes 4 servings.

Mix up your own quick tartar sauce!
Combine 1/2 cup mayonnaise, 2 tablespoons sweet
pickle relish and one tablespoon lemon juice.
Chill until serving time.

Snacks & Sandwiches to Share

Salsa Joes

Jess Brunink
Whitehall, MI

This is a quick go-to meal! When you have had a busy day,
it takes just a little bit of time and dinner is on the table.

1 lb. ground turkey
1/4 c. onion, diced
1 c. favorite salsa
salt to taste
4 to 6 hamburger buns, split

In a skillet over medium heat, brown turkey with onion. Stir in salsa; season with salt. Simmer for 10 minutes, stirring occasionally. Serve turkey mixture spooned onto buns. Makes 4 to 6 servings.

Homemade Salsa

Darrell Lawry
Kissimmee, FL

I keep the ingredients for this salsa on hand for a fiesta anytime.
Delicious with tortilla chips...spoon it onto tacos, too.

28-oz. can petite diced tomatoes
28-oz. can crushed tomatoes, drained
4-oz. can diced green chiles
2 T. dried, chopped onions
1 T. cider vinegar
2 t. salt
1/2 t. onion powder
1/2 t. garlic powder

In a large bowl, combine diced tomatoes with juice and remaining ingredients; stir well. Cover and refrigerate for 8 hours, or overnight. Makes about 7 cups.

A festive container for tortilla chips in a jiffy! Simply tie a knot
in each corner of a brightly colored bandanna, then tuck
a bowl into the center.

Fiesta Corn Dip

Joan Baker
Westland, MI

I got this recipe from a friend many years ago. Such an easy and delicious dip! Serve with crackers, tortilla or corn chips.

2 15-1/4 oz. cans fiesta corn
with sweet peppers, drained
2 c. mayonnaise
12-oz. pkg. shredded Colby
Jack cheese

4-oz. can diced jalapeño peppers,
drained
1/2 c. red pepper, chopped
1/4 c. shredded Parmesan cheese
1 T. hot pepper sauce

Combine all ingredients in a large bowl; mix well. Spread in a lightly greased 2-quart casserole dish. Bake, uncovered, at 350 degrees for about 30 minutes, until bubbly and cheese is melted. Makes 10 servings.

Now and then, it's good to pause in our pursuit of
happiness and just be happy.
–Guillaume Apollinaire

Snacks & Sandwiches to Share

Cuppa Wings

Marcia Marcoux
Charlton, MA

A new acquaintance shared this recipe and it has been a favorite with family & friends. Sometimes we grill them instead of broiling.

1 c. brown sugar, packed
1 c. sugar

1 c. low-sodium soy sauce
5 lbs. chicken wings, separated

Combine sugars and soy sauce in a very large bowl; mix well. Add wings; cover and refrigerate for at least one hour. Arrange wings on a large rimmed baking sheet. Drain marinade into a saucepan and bring to a boil for 5 minutes; cool. Bake wings, uncovered, at 300 degrees for 2 to 2-1/2 hours, turning wings and brushing with marinade. Place pan under the broiler; broil until wings are crisp. Serves 6 to 8.

Stovetop Lil' Sausages

Lori Simmons
Princeville, IL

A favorite! Transfer to a slow cooker to keep them warm.

1/2 c. brown sugar, packed
1/4 c. catsup
2 T. Dijon mustard

14-oz. pkg. mini cocktail
   sausages

Combine brown sugar, catsup and mustard in a large saucepan. Bring to a boil over medium heat. Add sausages; reduce heat to medium-low and simmer for 15 to 20 minutes. Sauce will be thin. To thicken, allow to cool and then reheat until warm. Serves 6 to 8.

Stir up a creamy dip for fresh fruit! Add 1/4 cup sugar and 2 teaspoons vanilla extract to a 16-ounce container sour cream; mix well and chill. Serve with apple slices, grapes and strawberries.

Beckie's Bean Dip

Beckie Apple
Grannis, AR

Wondering what to do with the last of your home-cooked pinto beans?
Whip up this easy bean dip! Serve with corn chips or crisp crackers.

1 c. cooked pinto beans
1/2 t. dried, flaked onions
1/2 t. chili powder
1/4 t. garlic powder

1/8 t. red pepper flakes
1/8 t. pepper
1/2 c. finely shredded Cheddar
   cheese

In a large bowl, mash beans well. Add seasonings and mix well; mix
in cheese. Microwave for 2 minutes, or until heated through. Makes
6 servings.

Corn Chip Pie Dip

Mel Chencharick
Julian, PA

My family loves to try different dips. I just had to try this one, and I'm
so glad I did! It's tasty and simple. If you like, top the hot dip with a
spoonful of your favorite salsa. Serve with scoop-type corn chips to
enjoy every bite.

16-oz. container sour cream
8-oz. pkg. cream cheese,
   softened and cubed

15-oz. can chili without beans
8-oz. pkg. shredded Cheddar
   cheese

In a large bowl, mix together sour cream and cream cheese. Spread
evenly in an 8" cast-iron skillet. Top with chili, spreading evenly.
Sprinkle with shredded cheese. Bake, uncovered, at 375 degrees for
25 minutes, until bubbly and cheese is melted. Makes 6 servings.

Snacks & Sandwiches to Share

Sour Cream Chicken Enchiladas
Susan Geisel
Hogansville, GA

I got this recipe from a friend, who got it from another friend, who got it forty years ago from the Atlanta Journal-Constitution newspaper. It's always good and can be served as an appetizer, sliced into segments, or as a meal.

3 c. cooked chicken, shredded
8-oz. container sour cream
1/2 c. onion, chopped
8-oz. pkg. shredded Mexican-
 blend cheese, divided

10 8-inch flour tortillas
16-oz. jar favorite salsa

In a large bowl, mix chicken, sour cream, onion and 1/2 cup cheese. Spoon mixture evenly down the center of tortillas and roll up. Arrange enchiladas in a lightly greased 13"x9" baking pan. Top with salsa and remaining cheese. Bake, uncovered, at 350 degrees for 15 to 20 minutes, until bubbly and heated through. Makes 5 to 6 servings.

Mix up a pitcher of mock margaritas! In a blender, combine a 6-ounce can of frozen limeade concentrate, 1/4 to 1/2 cup orange juice and 4 cups ice cubes. Process until well blended and ice cubes are evenly crushed. Pour into salt-rimmed glasses and enjoy.

Riverwalk Guacamole

Kathleen Craig
Burlington, WI

My daughter and I were visiting San Antonio, Texas, where we enjoyed guacamole made fresh, right at our restaurant table. I tried to remember their ingredients and added our favorites. I like to serve chopped jalapeños on the side, for everyone to add as they like.

2 T. orange juice
2 T. lemon or lime juice
1-1/4 c. frozen avocado chunks, thawed
1/4 c. onion, chopped

2 T. fresh cilantro, chopped
1 t. clove garlic, minced
Optional: chopped jalapeño peppers
salt to taste

Combine fruit juices in a bowl. Add avocado and chop coarsely. Add onion, cilantro and garlic; mix well. Have favorite chopped peppers in another bowl available for individuals to mix to taste. Add salt for individual taste as well. Makes 6 servings.

Cheesy quesadillas are quick and filling...great as a snack or paired with soup. Sprinkle a flour tortilla with shredded cheese, top with another tortilla and toast lightly in a skillet until the cheese melts. Cut into wedges and serve with your favorite salsa.

No-Fuss Soups & Breads

Oh-So Easy Taco Soup

Angie Whitmore
Farmington, UT

Busy day ahead? In the morning, assemble this soup in the slow cooker...it'll be ready for dinner when you are. Serve with tortilla chips or quesadillas.

2 14-1/2 oz. cans diced tomatoes
15-oz. can chili with beans
15-oz. can black beans, drained
   and rinsed
15-oz. can corn
8-oz. can tomato sauce

1/2 c. beef broth
1 T. taco seasoning mix,
   or to taste
Garnish: sour cream, shredded
   Cheddar cheese

In a blender, purée tomatoes with juice; pour into a lightly greased 4-quart slow cooker. Add remaining ingredients except garnish; stir to combine. Cover and cook on low setting for 6 to 8 hours. Top servings with sour cream and shredded cheese. Makes 4 to 6 servings.

If a recipe calls for canned tomatoes, take advantage of Mexican style with green onions, Italian style with basil and garlic or zesty chili style. Seasonings are already added...fewer ingredients for you to buy and measure!

No-Fuss Soups & Breads

Steakhouse Potato Soup

Audra Vanhorn-Sorey
Columbia, NC

*Slow-cooker easy...steakhouse style and good to the last drop!
If you have any leftovers, this soup will freeze well in freezer
bags for up to four months.*

30-oz. pkg. frozen shredded
    hashbrowns
3 14-oz. cans chicken broth
10-3/4 oz. can cream of
    chicken soup
1/2 c. onion, chopped

1/4 t. pepper
8-oz. pkg. cream cheese,
    softened and cubed
Garnish: shredded cheese, sour
    cream, crumbled bacon,
    chopped fresh chives

In a 5-quart slow cooker, combine hashbrowns, chicken broth, chicken soup, onion and pepper; stir well. Cover and cook on low setting for 6 to 8 hours. Stir in cream cheese one hour before serving. Garnish servings with desired toppings. Serves 6.

Best tip ever for success in the kitchen! Read the recipe the whole way through and make sure you have everything you'll need before you begin cooking.

Hearty Vegetable Soup

Ginny Watson
Scranton, PA

Mom used to make the most delicious vegetable soup for us, spending a lot of time chopping all the fresh vegetables. I think mine is almost as good as hers...with lots less work!

24-oz. pkg. frozen mixed
   vegetables
10-oz. pkg. frozen diced onions,
   celery & peppers
14-1/2 oz. can petite diced
   tomatoes

32-oz. container beef broth
15-oz. can tomato sauce
1 t. Italian seasoning
salt and pepper to taste
1 c. ditalini pasta, uncooked

In a Dutch oven, combine all frozen vegetables and tomatoes with juice; add beef broth, tomato sauce, seasonings and pasta. Bring to a boil over medium heat; reduce heat to medium-low. Cover and simmer for 20 to 30 minutes, stirring occasionally, until vegetables and pasta are tender. Makes 6 servings.

Fresh vegetables are only nutritious if they're used promptly, so don't hesitate to use frozen vegetables instead. Simmer in chicken broth for extra flavor, drain and top with butter. Or add them, still frozen, to a simmering pot of soup or a boiling pasta pot.

No-Fuss Soups & Breads

Bean & Sausage Soup

Brittany Kiesler
Corydon, IN

I love good old bean & bacon soup in the red & white can. I have fond memories of eating it as a child, especially when I wasn't feeling well. This recipe reminds me of a heartier version of that soup. It's very easy and great for fall and winter...simple to make in a slow cooker. Serve with cornbread.

32-oz. pkg. frozen diced potatoes
14-oz. pkg. skinless smoked
    pork sausage, halved
    lengthwise and sliced into
    half-moons

4 16-oz. cans Great Northern
    beans
2 to 3 carrots, peeled and diced
2 cubes chicken bouillon
pepper to taste

In a 5-quart slow cooker, combine all ingredients except pepper. Cover with water, filling crock 2/3 full. Cover and cook on high setting for 5 to 6 hours, or on low setting for 7 to 8 hours. Season with pepper and serve. Makes 8 servings.

Quick Beer Bread

Emily Martin
Toronto, Ontario

Tasty and super-easy...bake up a loaf to serve with hot soup.

3 c. self-rising flour
12-oz. can regular or
    non-alcoholic beer

3 T. sugar
1/4 c. butter, melted

Combine flour, beer and sugar; mix well. Pour batter into a greased 9"x5" loaf pan. Bake at 350 degrees for 40 minutes. Drizzle melted butter over loaf; bake 15 minutes more. Makes one loaf.

In my grandmother's house
there was always chicken soup
And talk of the old country...

–Louis Simpson

Ash's Delectable Chicken Soup

Ashley Phillips
Rayland, OH

So good on a cold day...without a doubt, the best soup I've ever had.

1/2 c. butter
1 c. onion, chopped
12-1/2 oz. can chunk chicken, drained
14-1/2 oz. can sliced carrots, drained

1 t. garlic & pepper seasoning
1 t. Italian seasoning
12-oz. pkg. extra-wide or Kluski egg noodles, uncooked
48-oz. container chicken broth

Melt butter in a soup pot over medium heat; cook onion for 3 to 4 minutes. Add chicken, carrots, seasonings and uncooked noodles; add enough broth to cover everything. Bring to a boil; reduce heat to medium-low. Simmer for 20 to 30 minutes, stirring occasionally, until noodles are done. Serves 4 to 6.

Bouillon cubes are an easy substitute for canned broth. To make one cup of broth, dissolve a bouillon cube in one cup of boiling water. Try soup base for a richer flavor. Easy to keep on hand... saves space in the pantry!

No-Fuss Soups & Breads

Quick & Easy Drop Biscuits

Beckie Apple
Grannis, AR

We love homemade bread of any kind, but time is usually a factor. This quick & easy biscuit recipe is great for our busy lifestyle.

2 c. all-purpose flour
2 T. sugar
1 T. baking powder
1/2 t. salt

1/4 c. chilled butter, chipped
   into small pieces
1 c. milk

In a large bowl, combine flour, sugar, baking powder and salt; mix well. Cut in butter with a pastry blender or knife until crumbly. Add milk; stir until a soft batter forms. Drop batter by 1/4 cupfuls onto a greased baking sheet, using a large cookie scoop. Bake at 450 degrees for 18 to 22 minutes, until golden. Makes 8 biscuits.

Chicken Spaetzle Soup

Kelly Alderson
Erie, PA

Grandma's old-fashioned chicken soup...but quick to make! Add a sprinkle of dried parsley and thyme, if you like.

10-oz. pkg. spaetzle egg
   dumplings, uncooked
2 T. butter
10-oz. pkg. frozen diced onions,
   carrots and celery

2 10-3/4 oz. cans cream of
   chicken soup
3 c. water
9-oz. pkg. cooked chicken
   strips, sliced

Cook spaetzle according to package directions; drain. Meanwhile, melt butter in a large saucepan over medium heat. Add frozen vegetables and cook for about 4 minutes, until tender. Add remaining ingredients; cook over medium heat for 10 minutes. Reduce heat to low; simmer for 15 minutes, or until vegetables are tender. Stir in cooked spaetzle; simmer for 3 minutes. Serves 6 to 8.

Drain and rinse canned beans before using,
for fresher flavor and less sodium.

Mary's Cheese Soup

Marian Forck
Chamois, MO

*You are going to love this soup! My friend makes this soup
and it is so good, I had to ask her for the recipe.*

6 c. water
4 cubes chicken bouillon
1 c. celery, diced
1/2 c. onion, diced
2 c. potatoes, peeled and chopped
20-oz. pkg. frozen chopped
 broccoli, cauliflower
 and carrots

Optional: 10-oz. pkg. frozen
 chopped broccoli
2 10-3/4 oz. cans cream of
 chicken soup
1 to 1-1/2 lbs. pasteurized
 process cheese, cubed
Optional: 1 c. cooked ham,
 chopped

In a large soup pot, combine water, bouillon cubes, celery, onion and
potatoes. Bring to a boil over high heat; reduce heat to medium-low
and simmer for 20 to 25 minutes. Meanwhile, in a separate saucepan
over medium heat, cook frozen vegetables according package directions;
drain. In another saucepan over low heat, combine chicken soup and
cheese. Cook, stirring often, until cheese is melted. Add vegetables and
soup mixture to broth mixture in soup pot. Add ham, if using; stir well
and heat through. Makes 8 servings.

Keep frozen chopped onions, peppers and other veggies on hand.
They'll thaw quickly so you can assemble a recipe in a snap...
no peeling, chopping or dicing needed!

Quick & Easy Corn Chowder

Audrey Stapleford
Merrimack, NH

Good for lunch or dinner on a stormy day, served with your favorite bread. I like to add a dash of smoky paprika and a bit of crushed dried tarragon to taste.

1 baking potato, peeled and diced
14-3/4 oz. can cream-style corn
10-3/4 oz. can cream of
   chicken soup
16-oz. container half-and-half
2 to 3 t. butter

1/4 c. onion, chopped
1 stalk celery, finely diced
1 carrot, peeled and finely diced
1 slice pasteurized process
   cheese, chopped

In a large saucepan, cover potato with water. Cook over medium heat until tender, about 10 minutes; drain. Reduce heat to low. Add corn, chicken soup and half-and-half; stir well. Meanwhile, melt butter in a small skillet over medium heat; sauté onion, celery and carrot and add to potato mixture. Heat through over low to medium heat, but do not boil. Add cheese; simmer gently for several minutes and serve. Makes 4 servings.

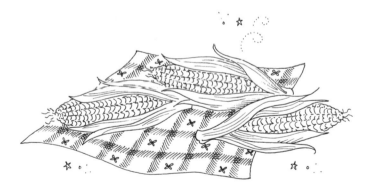

Save odds & ends of leftover veggies in a freezer bag. Before you know it, you'll have enough for a big pot of hearty soup. Add a can of tomato sauce and/or chicken broth, and favorite seasonings to taste. Cover and simmer over low heat. Delicious and economical!

Spinach-Sausage Tortellini Soup

Jean DeGroff
Raleigh, NC

I first sampled a soup like this at a luncheon where I worked at a cancer care center. Everyone brought something in to share with our patients. I have altered it somewhat to my liking and now it's a family favorite. I use half hot and half sweet sausage so it is not so spicy, but adjust to your own preference. Dried, fresh or frozen tortellini may be used.

2 T. olive oil
4 pork sausage links, removed
   from casings
2 to 3 cloves garlic, finely
   chopped
2 32-oz. containers
   chicken broth

14-1/2 oz. can stewed tomatoes
6-oz. pkg fresh baby spinach,
   stems removed
12-oz. pkg. cheese tortellini,
   uncooked

Heat oil in a stockpot over medium heat. Crumble sausage into pot and cook until nearly browned. Add garlic and cook until browned; drain. Add chicken broth, stewed tomatoes with juice and spinach. Reduce heat to medium-low. Simmer for about one hour, stirring occasionally. Shortly before serving time, return to a boil; add tortellini and cook according to package directions. Makes 6 to 8 servings.

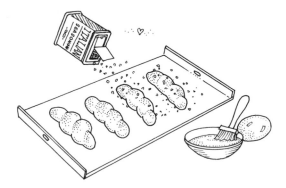

Twisty bread sticks are a tasty go-with for soup. Brush refrigerated bread stick dough with a little beaten egg and dust with Italian seasoning, then pop in the oven until toasty. Yummy!

No-Fuss Soups & Breads

Those Garlic Biscuits

Caroline Britt
Cleveland, TX

These are so much like those "restaurant biscuits" that everyone loves. They're great with soups, stews and chili.

2 c. all-purpose flour
2 T. garlic powder
1 T. baking powder
1 t. salt
3/4 t. sugar

1/2 c. butter, melted
1-1/2 c. buttermilk, or more
   as needed
8-oz. pkg. shredded Cheddar
   cheese

In a large bowl, mix together flour, garlic, baking powder, salt and sugar. Add melted butter and stir until mixture is crumbly. Stir in buttermilk; fold in cheese. If too dry, add a little more buttermilk to form a soft dough. Using a large cookie scoop, drop dough by 1/4 cupfuls onto a greased baking sheet. Bake at 350 degrees for 26 to 28 minutes, until golden. Makes one dozen.

Cheesy Wild Rice Soup

Carolyn Gochenaur
Howe, IN

This soup was brought to my sister by a friend after she'd had one of her babies during the cold winter months of northwest Minnesota. It has been a family favorite of her family and mine for many years.

1 c. wild rice, uncooked
4 c. water
1/2 lb. bacon, diced
3/4 c. frozen chopped onions
4 c. whole milk

2 10-3/4 oz. cans cream of
   potato soup
2 c. pasteurized process cheese,
   cubed

Combine rice and water in a large saucepan over medium heat. Bring to a boil; simmer for 45 minutes, stirring often. Do not allow to cook dry; add a little water, if needed. Meanwhile, cook bacon in a stockpot over medium heat until partially done. Add onion and cook until tender; drain. Stir in milk, potato soup and cheese. Cook and stir until heated through and cheese is melted; do not boil. Stir in cooked rice and serve. Serves 8 to 10.

Enchilada Soup

Taylor Johnston
Beavercreek, OR

Top each bowl with whatever you like on your tacos...fresh cilantro,
shredded cheese, chopped tomatoes, crushed tortilla chips. Yum!

16-oz. can refried beans
15-1/2 oz. can black beans,
 drained
15-1/4 oz. can corn, drained
14-oz. can chicken broth
12-oz. can shredded chicken,
 drained

10-oz. can red enchilada sauce
1 c. favorite salsa
1 t. ground cumin
1 T. taco seasoning mix
hot pepper sauce to taste
Garnish: shredded cheese,
 chopped fresh cilantro

In a 5-quart slow cooker, combine all ingredients except garnish. Mix
gently. Cover and cook on high setting for 4 hours. Garnish servings as
desired. Makes 6 servings.

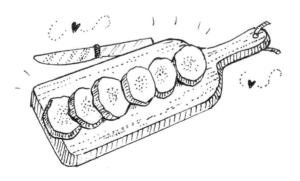

If a recipe calls for cooked chicken, baked ham or roast beef,
order thick-sliced meat at the deli counter. Buy just
what you need...it's ready to cube or chop as needed.

Pappy's Cornbread

Gwen Hudson
Madison Heights, VA

Many years ago, a local family eatery had this tasty cornbread on the menu. I was told that the owner's grandmother made this for her grandfather, whose nickname was Pappy.

6-oz. pkg. country-style
   cornbread mix
1/2 c. white cornmeal
1 t. baking powder

2 eggs, beaten
1/2 c. oil
16-oz. container sour cream
8-1/4 oz. can cream-style corn

In a large bowl, combine dry cornbread mix, cornmeal, baking powder, eggs and oil; mix well. Stir in sour cream and corn. Pour batter into a 9" round baking pan that has been sprayed with non-stick vegetable spray. Bake at 400 degrees for 30 to 40 minutes, until golden. Cut into wedges to serve. Makes 6 to 8 servings.

Grandma's old cast-iron skillet is perfect for baking crisp, golden cornbread. Before you mix up the batter, drop a tablespoon of bacon drippings or oil into the skillet and preheat it in the oven. When the batter is ready, the skillet will be too.

Shortcut Split Pea Soup

Mary Lou Thomas
Portland, ME

My mother always made the best split pea soup. She'd begin by soaking the dried peas and made her own chicken broth, too. I still love a cup of split pea soup in chilly weather, but this way is faster.

3 c. water
2 t. chicken bouillon granules
1/2 t. dried parsley
1/2 t. dried thyme
4 stalks celery, sliced and
    leaves reserved

1/2 c. baby carrots, thinly sliced
2 11-1/2 oz. cans split pea soup
1 c. cooked ham, diced
Optional: shredded Parmesan
    cheese

In a large saucepan over medium heat, combine water, bouillon granules and seasonings. Bring to a boil. Add celery and carrots; reduce heat to medium-low and simmer for 5 to 8 minutes. Stir in chopped celery leaves, pea soup and ham; heat through. Top servings with Parmesan cheese, if desired. Makes 5 servings.

A jar of dried, minced onions can be a real time-saver! In soups and stews, just substitute one tablespoon of dried, minced onion for every 1/3 cup diced fresh onion.

No-Fuss Soups & Breads

5-Ingredient Cheese Soup

Emilie Britton
New Bremen, OH

This is a simple soup I like to make with leftover ham or turkey.

2 10-3/4 oz. cans cream of
   potato soup
10-3/4 oz. can cream of
   celery soup
1-1/4 c. milk

8-oz. pkg. shredded Cheddar
   cheese
1/2 to 1 c. cooked ham or
   turkey, diced

Combine all ingredients in a 4-quart slow cooker and stir well. Cover and cook on low setting for 2 to 4 hours, until hot and bubbly. Serves 4.

Quick Tomato Soup

Joanne Novellino
Bayville, NJ

This is the fastest and tastiest tomato soup I know!

40-oz. jar tomato-basil
   pasta sauce
1/2 c. evaporated milk

1/4 c. half-and-half
1/3 c. chicken broth

Combine tomato sauce, milk and half-and-half in a blender. Add chicken broth to tomato sauce jar; swirl to clean out jar and add to blender; process until puréed. Transfer mixture to a saucepan; heat through over medium heat and serve. Makes 4 servings.

Grilled cheese...tomato soup's perfect partner. Get out Grandma's cast-iron skillet for the tastiest, toastiest sandwiches. Cast iron provides even heat distribution for speedy cooking and crisp golden crusts.

SHORTCUTS TO
Grandma's Best
RECIPES

Winter's Best Bean Soup

Kathy Grashoff
Fort Wayne, IN

This slow-cooker soup is hearty and flavorful...made with very little effort. I like to serve it ladled over slices of toasted Italian bread, drizzled with olive oil.

10 c. chicken broth
3 15-1/2 oz. cans cannellini
   beans, drained and rinsed
14-1/2 oz. can diced tomatoes
10-oz. pkg. frozen crinkle-cut
   carrots, drained

6 slices bacon, crisply cooked
   and crumbled
1 c. frozen chopped onions
2 t. garlic, minced
1 sprig fresh rosemary
1 t. pepper

Combine all ingredients in a 5-quart slow cooker; stir to blend. Cover and cook on low setting for 7 to 8 hours. Discard rosemary sprig before serving. Makes 8 to 10 servings.

Tina's Buttermilk Biscuits

Tina Goodpasture
Meadowview, VA

My Granny Hudson always had something to eat on her kitchen table. She was the best cook, and her kitchen always smelled so good. I never heard her say a harsh word to anybody! I sure miss her morning bread.

4 c. self-rising soft-wheat flour
1 c. shortening

1-3/4 c. buttermilk

Place flour in a large bowl; cut in shortening with a pastry blender until crumbly. Add buttermilk; stir just until moistened. Turn dough out onto a lightly floured surface; knead lightly 5 to 6 times. Pat or roll dough to 3/4 inch thickness. Cut with a 1-1/2 inch round cutter; arrange on 3 lightly greased baking sheets. Bake at 425 degrees for 12 to 14 minutes, until lightly golden. Makes 3 dozen.

No-Fuss
Soups & Breads

Gram's Hodgepodge Soup

Sandy Coffey
Cincinnati, OH

An easy, lazy kind of supper, especially on the cooler days of fall and winter. Delicious with slices of garlic bread.

1 to 1-1/2 lbs. ground beef chuck
5 10-3/4 oz. cans minestrone
  soup
31-oz. can pork & beans in
  tomato sauce
10-3/4 oz. can tomato soup
1-1/4 c. water
1 T. Worcestershire sauce
1 to 2 t. dried, minced onions
salt and garlic salt to taste

Brown beef in a stockpot over medium heat; drain well. Stir in remaining ingredients; reduce heat to low. Simmer for 30 minutes, stirring occasionally. Makes 6 to 8 servings.

Ladle portions of soup into small plastic freezer containers, add the lid and freeze. Whenever you need a quick-fix lunch or dinner, simply uncover and microwave until hot.

Cream of Chicken-Rice Soup

Bethi Hendrickson
Danville, PA

This is a wonderful, easy-to-make soup on cold winter nights when you need a quick dinner. Serve with a salad...supper is complete!

1/2 c. butter
1 c. baby carrots, thinly sliced
Optional: 1 c. onion, diced
1/2 c. all-purpose flour
4 c. chicken broth
8.8-oz. pkg. ready-to-serve
   chicken-flavored rice

1/2 c. long-cooking rice,
   uncooked
2 c. cooked chicken, shredded
1 qt. fat-free half-and-half

Melt butter in a soup pot over medium heat; add carrots and onion, if using. Cook for 10 minutes, or until tender. Sprinkle with flour. Cook for 5 minutes, stirring often, or until mixture is golden. Stir in chicken broth, cooked and uncooked rice. Simmer over low heat for 20 to 25 minutes, until rice is tender, stirring occasionally. Stir in chicken and half-and-half; heat through, but do not boil. Makes 6 to 8 servings.

A roast chicken from the deli is the busy cook's secret ingredient! The chicken is already cooked and ready for whatever recipe you decide to make.

No-Fuss Soups & Breads

Sour Cream Onion Biscuits

Molly Ebert
Columbus, IN

*These tender biscuits were a happy accident! When I realized I didn't
have sour cream on hand for sour cream biscuits, I subbed the
only thing I had on hand...French onion chip dip!*

2 c. biscuit baking mix
1/4 c. milk

8-oz. container French onion
   sour cream dip

Combine all ingredients in a large bowl; stir until a soft dough forms.
Drop dough in 6 mounds onto a lightly greased baking sheet. Bake at
450 degrees for 10 to 12 minutes, until light golden. Makes 6 biscuits.

Tiny Cream Cheese Biscuits

Julie Perkins
Anderson, IN

*A tried & true recipe from the wonderful cooks at church.
Serve them hot from the oven...scrumptious!*

8-oz. pkg. cream cheese,
   softened

1/2 c. margarine, softened
1 c. self-rising flour

In a large bowl, beat cream cheese and margarine with an electric mixer
on medium speed for 2 minutes, or until creamy. Gradually add flour;
beat on low speed just until blended. Spoon batter into ungreased mini
muffin cups, filling full. Bake at 400 degrees for 15 minutes, or until
golden. Serve warm. Makes 1-1/2 dozen.

Honey butter is delectable melting on warm bread.
Simply blend 2/3 cup honey with 1/2 cup softened butter.

Tex-Mex Chicken Soup

Wendy Ball
Battle Creek, MI

This soup can be made in no time! It's a quick way to use up rotisserie chicken and whatever else you have on hand. If you don't have salsa, just use a can of diced tomatoes and a small can of diced mild green chiles. No vegetable broth? Either chicken broth or vegetable cocktail juice can be used.

1-1/2 lb. deli rotisserie chicken,
   diced or shredded
32-oz. container vegetable broth
14-1/2 oz. can diced tomatoes
16-oz. jar favorite salsa
15-1/2 oz. can black beans,
   drained or rinsed
15-1/4 oz. can corn, drained,
   or 10-oz. pkg. frozen corn

1/4 c. enchilada sauce
1 c. water
1-1/4 oz. pkg. taco
   seasoning mix
Garnish: shredded Cheddar
   cheese, sour cream,
   tortilla chips

In a large Dutch oven or soup pot, combine all ingredients except garnish. Stir well. Cook over medium heat until heated through, stirring occasionally. Serve with cheese, sour cream and tortilla chips. Serves 8 to 10.

Wrap and freeze small amounts of leftover cheeses. They may become crumbly when thawed, but will still be delicious in hot dishes.

Carter's Favorite Chili

Jenny Bishoff
Oakland, MD

My son Carter has loved chili since he was a toddler, and I love making it for him! This one is his favorite because there are no tomato chunks. It's so easy, it's almost not a recipe!

1 lb. ground beef
1 onion, diced
14-1/2 oz. can petite diced
   tomatoes, or 15-oz. can
   tomato sauce

15-oz. can mild chili beans
1-1/4 oz. pkg. chili
   seasoning mix

In a Dutch oven over medium heat, cook beef with onion until beef is browned and onion is soft; drain. Add tomatoes with liquid or tomato sauce, beans with liquid and chili seasoning. Stir in enough water to thin to desired consistency. Simmer over medium-low heat for at least 30 minutes, to allow flavors to blend. May also combine all ingredients in a 4-quart slow cooker; cover and cook on low setting for 4 to 6 hours. Makes 6 servings.

Serve it Cincinnati-style! For 2-way chili, ladle chili over a bowl of spaghetti. For 3-way, top chili and spaghetti with shredded cheese. For 4-way, spoon diced onions on top of the cheese...add chili beans to the stack for 5-way. Delicious, any way you choose!

Spicy Potato & Corn Chowder

Tiffany Jones
Batesville, AR

One snowy winter day, I was craving a hearty chowder. I had seen a few soup recipes that called for using an au gratin potato mix, so I decided to create my own recipe. Oh my...it was delicious! Such a comforting meal.

1 onion, chopped
11-oz. can white shoepeg corn
10-oz. can diced tomatoes with
   green chiles
7-oz. can chopped green chiles
7.7-oz. pkg. au gratin
   potatoes mix

2 c. water
2 c. whipping cream
1 t. salt
1/2 t. pepper
8 slices fully cooked bacon,
   warmed and chopped

Add all ingredients except bacon to a large pot, including cheese mix from potato package. Bring to a boil over medium-high heat; reduce heat to medium-low. Simmer for 30 minutes, stirring occasionally. Stir bacon into soup and serve. Makes 8 servings.

Longing for Grandma's old-fashioned homemade egg noodles? Try frozen homestyle egg noodles from your grocer's frozen food section.

No-Fuss Soups & Breads

Slow-Cooker Clam Chowder

*Dawn Thompson
Saint Peters, MO*

*I have traveled through Maine and this is the best clam chowder
I have ever tasted. Perfect for chilly-day meals...let your
slow cooker do all the work!*

1/4 c. butter
3/4 c. onion, chopped
6-1/2 oz. can chopped clams,
   drained

2 10-oz. cans clam chowder
3 10-3/4 oz. cans cream of
   potato soup
1 qt. half-and-half

Melt butter in a skillet over medium heat; sauté onion and clams for
10 minutes. In a 4-quart slow cooker, whisk together soups and
half-and-half; stir in onion mixture. Cover and cook on low setting
for 4 to 6 hours. Makes 4 servings.

Zesty Tomato-Crab Bisque

*Tina Wright
Atlanta, GA*

*I love to serve mugs of this tasty soup to everyone who's
coming in out of the cold.*

2 19-oz. cans hearty
   tomato soup
7-oz. can chopped green chiles
1 c. whipping cream

1 t. seafood seasoning
3/4 c. real or imitation crabmeat,
   flaked

In a 3-quart saucepan, combine tomato soup and chiles. Bring to a boil
over medium heat. Reduce heat to low; whisk in cream and seasoning.
Simmer for several minutes, just until heated through; do not boil. Stir
in crabmeat. Ladle soup into small soup bowls. Makes 4 to 6 servings.

Instant mashed potato flakes are
handy for thickening soups...great for
breading chicken and fish, too.

Barb's Tomato Soup

Barbara Klein
Newburgh, IN

I love tomato soup, but canned tomato soup needs a little pick-me-up. Here's my tasty version...it goes very well with a grilled cheese sandwich.

2 T. butter
2 stalks celery, diced
1/2 onion, diced
2 T. all-purpose flour
1-1/2 c. water
14-1/2 oz. can diced tomatoes

10-3/4 oz. can tomato soup
1 t. Worcestershire sauce
1 t. dried dill weed
1 t. dried parsley
salt and pepper to taste
Optional: croutons

Melt butter in a saucepan over medium heat. Add celery and onion; cook and stir until tender. Sprinkle with flour; cook and stir for 2 minutes. Stir in water; simmer until thickened. Add tomatoes with juice, tomato soup, Worcestershire sauce and seasonings; bring to a light boil. Simmer until heated through and thickened. Serve with croutons, if desired. Makes 4 servings.

Top bowls of soup with crunchy cheese toasts. Brush thin slices of French bread lightly with olive oil. Broil for 2 to 3 minutes, until golden. Turn over and sprinkle with shredded Parmesan cheese and Italian seasoning. Broil another 2 to 3 minutes, until cheese melts. Yum!

No-Fuss Soups & Breads

Creamy Potato Soup

Jenny Bishoff
Oakland, MD

*One day, I had a few items in my pantry and fridge to use up,
including two random potatoes and some limp celery. Turns out,
this potato soup was a great way to make do!*

2 T. butter
1 onion, chopped
2 stalks celery, chopped
2 potatoes, peeled and diced
4 c. chicken broth

4-oz. pkg. flavored instant
   mashed potato flakes
Garnish: shredded Cheddar
   cheese, crumbled bacon,
   chopped fresh chives

Melt butter in a skillet over medium heat; sauté onion, celery and
potatoes until softened. Add chicken broth and simmer until potatoes
are tender. Stir in instant potatoes, adding a little more broth, if needed;
heat through. Serve topped with shredded cheese, crumbled bacon and
chopped chives. Makes 4 to 6 servings.

A pot of chicken soup and a cheery bouquet of posies are sure
pick-me-ups for a friend who is feeling under the weather.

Chicken Fajita Soup

Tiffany Jones
Batesville, AR

I am a big soup fan. I came up with this when I was out of taco seasoning...it was delicious! There's never any left when I bring it to potlucks. For convenience, I like to use deli rotisserie chicken.

1 c. cooked chicken, diced
14-1/2 oz. can diced tomatoes
   with green chiles
14-1/2 oz. diced tomatoes
15-1/2 oz. can black beans,
   drained

14-1/2 oz. can chicken broth
1-1/4 oz. packet fajita
   seasoning mix
1-oz. pkg. ranch seasoning mix
Optional: salad tortilla strips

Combine all ingredients except optional tortilla strips in a large pot over medium heat; stir well. Bring to a boil. Reduce heat to medium-low; simmer for 15 minutes. Serve topped with tortilla strips, if desired. Makes 6 servings.

Bring out Grandma's cheery fruit or flower table linens for special family get-togethers. So pretty, and they will spark conversations about other special gatherings.

No-Fuss Soups & Breads

Best-Ever Cornbread

Barb Bargdill
Gooseberry Patch

Really tasty cornbread to serve with your favorite soup! Use fresh, frozen or canned corn...great for cleaning out the fridge. Use your favorite cast-iron skillet coated with bacon drippings, if you like.

8-1/2 oz. pkg. corn muffin mix
2 eggs, beaten
1/2 c. mayonnaise

1/4 c. butter, melted
1 c. corn, thawed if frozen

In a large bowl, stir together all ingredients; pour batter into a greased 9"x9" baking pan. Bake at 400 degrees for 25 to 28 minutes, until golden; cut into squares and serve. Makes 6 servings.

Slow-Cooker Potato Tot Soup

Judy Lange
Imperial, PA

Kids love this soup...it's really easy, so I love it too!

10-3/4 oz. can cream of
    mushroom soup
4 c. whole milk
1 t. salt
1 t. pepper

32-oz. pkg. frozen potato puffs
1-1/2 c. cooked ham, chopped
1 c. shredded Cheddar cheese
1/2 c. onion, chopped

Whisk together mushroom soup, milk and seasonings in a 6-quart slow cooker. Fold in remaining ingredients. Cover and cook on high setting for 3 to 3-1/2 hours, until bubbly and potato puffs are done. Thin with a little more milk, if desired. Makes 6 servings.

Separate frozen vegetables easily...add them to a colander and run hot water over them. Drain well and add to your recipe.

Cheesy Sausage Soup

Joyce Roebuck
Jacksonville, TX

This soup is so good on a cold, gloomy day...it warms the soul.
Use hot sausage if you like it a little bit spicy. This will
serve a good number of people.

1 lb. ground mild or hot
    pork sausage
1 green pepper, chopped
1 red pepper, chopped
1 c. frozen chopped onion
1 T. all-purpose flour
2 32-oz. containers
    chicken broth

32-oz. pkg. frozen diced
    hashbrown potatoes
10-oz. pkg. frozen corn
16-oz. pkg. pasteurized process
    cheese, cubed
1 c. sour cream

In a large Dutch oven over medium heat, brown sausage with peppers and onion for about 10 minutes. Drain; sprinkle with flour. Cook, stirring constantly, for 2 minutes. Gradually stir in chicken broth, hashbrowns and corn; bring to a boil. Reduce heat to medium-low. Simmer for 10 minutes, or until hashbrowns are tender. Add cheese and stir until melted. Stir in sour cream; heat through, but do not boil. Makes 8 to 10 servings.

Begin family meals with a gratitude circle...each person takes a moment to share something that he or she is thankful for that day. It's a sure way to put everyone in a cheerful mood!

No-Fuss Soups & Breads

Broccoli & Cheese Soup

Leona Krivda
Belle Vernon, PA

I love homemade soups! This is a good one that my family loves too. Add some warm bread or rolls and a crisp salad and you have a quick & easy meal.

32-oz. container low-sodium
   chicken broth
2 c. frozen shredded hashbrown
   potatoes
4 c. frozen chopped broccoli
Optional: 1 c. baby carrots, diced

2 c. milk
3 T. all-purpose flour
8-oz. pkg. pasteurized process
   cheese, cubed, or more
   to taste
salt and pepper to taste

In a large stockpot, combine chicken broth, hashbrowns, broccoli and carrots, if using. Bring to a boil over high heat; reduce heat to medium-low. Simmer for about 15 minutes, until vegetables are tender. In a bowl, blend milk and flour; add to vegetable mixture. Cook, stirring constantly, until soup thickens. Remove from heat and add cheese; stir well until cheese is melted and smooth. Season with salt and pepper. Makes 8 servings.

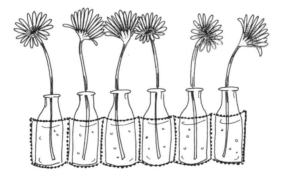

We gather simple pleasures like daisies by the way.
–Louisa May Alcott

Italian-Style Beef Stew

Liz Plotnick-Snay
Gooseberry Patch

We love this hearty stew in the slow cooker...it takes almost no effort at all! Warm up a loaf of garlic bread and dinner is served.

3 lbs. stew beef cubes
16-oz. pkg. frozen mixed Italian vegetables
1/4 c. frozen chopped onions

29-oz. can tomato sauce
1-1/2 oz. pkg. beef stew seasoning mix
1 T. Worcestershire sauce

Cut beef cubes into smaller pieces, if desired; add to a 6-quart slow cooker. Top with remaining ingredients; stir well. Cover and cook on low setting for 8 to 9 hours, or on high setting for 4 hours. Makes 6 to 8 servings.

Cast-Iron Garlic Rolls

Josh Logan
Victoria, TX

Soup in the slow cooker? Prep the rolls while it's simmering... you can have hot rolls for dinner. Delicious!

3 T. butter, melted
1/2 t. garlic powder
1/2 t. dried parsley

10 frozen yeast dinner rolls, thawed

In a small bowl, combine melted butter and seasonings. Dip each roll into butter mixture, coating completely; arrange in a greased 10" cast-iron skillet. Refrigerate remaining butter mixture. Cover with plastic wrap and let rise until double in size. Uncover; brush with remaining butter mixture. Bake at 350 degrees for 12 to 15 minutes, until golden. Makes 10 rolls.

Stir some alphabet pasta into a pot of vegetable soup...
you'll feel like a kid again!

No-Fuss Soups & Breads

Parmesan Garlic Bread

Mia Rossi
Charlotte, NC

Wonderful with soups and pasta dishes! I make up little containers of the butter mixture to freeze, then it just needs to thaw a bit and presto...garlic bread.

1/2 c. butter, softened
1/3 c. grated Parmesan cheese
1 T. garlic powder

1 t. dried parsley
1/2-lb. loaf French bread, cut
   into one-inch slices

In a bowl, combine butter, cheese and seasonings. Mix well; spread on bread slices. Reassemble loaf on a length of aluminum foil; wrap loaf, leaving top partially uncovered. Bake at 375 degrees for 15 to 20 minutes, until toasty and butter is melted. Serves 4 to 6.

Need some softened butter in a hurry? Grate chilled sticks of butter with a cheese grater...it will soften in just minutes.

Lisanne's Chicken Stew

Lisanne Miller
Wells, ME

Easy and tasty...everyone loves it! Serve with shredded Cheddar or mozzarella cheese and some warm crusty bread.

3 to 4 boneless, skinless chicken breasts
10-oz. pkg. frozen chopped broccoli
10-oz. pkg. frozen mixed vegetables
3 stalks celery, chopped

1/2 c. onion, chopped
1 T. garlic, minced
2 32-oz. containers chicken broth
1/2 c. water
16-oz. pkg. penne pasta, uncooked

In a 6-quart slow cooker, layer chicken breasts, all vegetables and garlic; pour chicken broth and water over all. Mix gently. Cover and cook on low setting for 5 to 6 hours, until chicken is tender. Remove chicken from crock; shred and return to crock. About 30 minutes before serving time, separately cook pasta according to package directions; drain. Spoon cooked pasta on top of stew; cover and let stand about 15 minutes before serving. Makes 4 to 6 servings.

Dress up a pot of soup with some tasty dumplings. Mix 2 cups biscuit baking mix with 3/4 cup milk...add a sprinkle of dried parsley, if you like. Drop batter into simmering soup by large spoonfuls. Cover and cook for about 15 minutes, until dumplings are set.

No-Fuss Soups & Breads

Busy-Day Beef & Veggie Soup

Shirley Howie
Foxboro, MA

This hearty soup is perfect for those busy weeknights, as it requires little prep time and can be left to simmer on its own. If it becomes too thick, just add a bit more water. Serve with warm, buttered rolls for a complete and satisfying meal!

1 lb. ground beef
28-oz. can diced tomatoes with
    basil, garlic & oregano
5 c. water

1-oz. pkg. onion soup mix
1-3/4 c. frozen mixed vegetables,
    thawed
1 c. elbow macaroni, uncooked

Brown beef in a large soup pot over medium heat; drain. Add tomatoes with juice, water and soup mix. Simmer, uncovered, over medium-low heat for one hour. Add vegetables and uncooked macaroni. Cook over medium heat for 15 minutes longer, or until vegetables and macaroni are tender. Makes 4 to 6 servings.

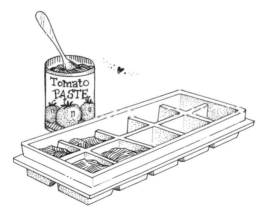

A spoonful of tomato paste adds rich flavor to stews and soups.
Freeze extra tomato paste in an ice cube tray, then pop out cubes
and store in a freezer bag. Frozen cubes can be dropped
right into simmering dishes.

Sloppy Silly Chili

Andrea Heyart
Savannah, TX

One night I was making a quick & easy chili, and realized that I was out of tomato sauce. Luckily I had a can of Sloppy Joe sauce in my pantry, so I used it instead. I've been making it that way ever since. Some accidents are just delicious! This makes quite a lot...leftovers can be frozen for an easy meal another day.

1 lb. ground beef
1 white onion, chopped
2 15-1/2 oz. cans chili beans
15-1/2 oz. can black beans
15-1/2 oz. can Sloppy Joe sauce
10-oz. can diced tomatoes with
   green chiles

2 to 3 t. chili powder
1/8 t. garlic powder
salt and pepper to taste
Garnish: shredded cheese, sour
   cream, crackers

In a Dutch oven over medium heat, brown beef with onion until beef is no longer pink and onion is translucent. Drain. Add undrained cans one at a time, stirring after each addition. Add seasonings and stir to combine. Bring to a low boil over medium heat; reduce heat to medium-low. Cover and simmer for 15 to 20 minutes, stirring occasionally, until warmed through. Add any additional seasonings if needed. Serve with desired toppings. Makes 10 to 12 servings.

A fun meal with friends...serve up a chili bar! Alongside a bubbling pot of chili, set out saltine crackers, shredded cheese, chopped onions and your favorite hot sauce. Sure to please all ages!

No-Fuss Soups & Breads

Penny's Spinach Cornbread

Penny Oswalt
Jonesboro, AR

I make this every year during football season, to serve with my homemade chili. I also make it for the first fall weather we have.

2 8-1/2 oz. pkgs. corn
  muffin mix
4 eggs, beaten
8-oz. pkg. cream cheese,
  softened
1 c. onion, chopped

10-oz. pkg. frozen chopped
  spinach, thawed and well
  drained
1 c. shredded fiesta-blend
  cheese
1 c. butter, melted

In a large bowl, mix together dry corn muffin mixes and remaining ingredients except shredded cheese and melted butter. Pour batter into a sprayed 13"x9" baking pan. Top with cheese; drizzle butter over all. Bake at 400 degrees for 30 to 45 minutes, until set and golden. Cut into squares. Serves 8 to 10

When chopping veggies, set the cutting board on a damp kitchen towel and it won't slip.

20-Minute Butternut Squash Soup

Kelly Serdynski Gray
Hedgesville, WV

This is our beginning-of-fall meal...using frozen cubed butternut squash really speeds it up! When we decorate for fall, this always comes to the dinner table that night, served up in mini pumpkins. It's so luxurious.

2 10-oz. pkgs. frozen cubed
   butternut squash, thawed
2 T. butter
1 yellow onion, finely diced
2 stalks celery, finely diced
2 c. chicken broth

2 c. whipping cream
2 t. garlic salt
1 t. pepper
1 t. dried sage
Optional: sour cream,
   pumpkin seeds

Add squash to a Dutch oven; set aside. Melt butter in a skillet over medium heat. Sauté onion and celery for about 5 minutes; add to squash along with chicken broth. Increase heat to medium-high and cook for 5 minutes. Stir in cream and seasonings. Heat through, about another 5 minutes. Purée soup in pan to desired consistency, using an immersion blender. Serve in bowls or mini pumpkins, topped with a dollop of sour cream and a sprinkle of pumpkin seeds, if desired. Serves 8.

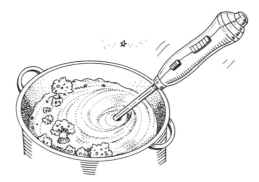

If a simmering pot of soup begins to burn on the bottom, just spoon the unburnt portion into another pan. Be careful not to scrape up the scorched part on the bottom. The burnt taste usually won't linger.

Easy-Peasy Salads & Sides

Ruth's Mixed Vegetable Casserole

Marcia Shaffer
Conneaut Lake, PA

Fifty years ago or more, my husband and I attended an Amish farm for dinner. This is one of the dishes our hostess Ruth served and we have loved it ever since. It is easy-peasy and delicious...even little kids like it.

10-oz. pkg. frozen mixed
    vegetables
10-3/4 oz. can cream of
    mushroom soup
1/2 t. dried marjoram
1/2 t. dried basil

Optional: 1/2 c. chopped onion,
    1/2 c. chopped celery
6-oz. pkg. chicken-flavored
    stuffing mix
1/2 c. butter, melted

Combine all ingredients except stuffing mix and melted butter in a greased 2-quart casserole dish; mix well. Combine stuffing mix and butter in a bowl; toss to mix and sprinkle on top. Bake, uncovered, at 350 degrees for 30 minutes, until heated through. Serves 6.

Easy iced tea is perfect with meals anytime. Fill a 2-quart pitcher with cold water and drop in 6 to 8 tea bags. Refrigerate for several hours. Discard tea bags; add sugar to taste and serve over ice.

Easy-Peasy Salads & Sides

Mexicali Salad

Kathy Grashoff
Fort Wayne, IN

Oh-so simple to make...delicious alongside tacos and burgers.

15-1/2 oz. can black beans,
    drained and rinsed
1 c. corn, thawed if frozen
3/4 c. roasted red peppers,
    drained and chopped
1/3 c. mild chipotle salsa or
    regular salsa

2 T. cider vinegar
1/2 c. red or yellow onion,
    chopped and divided
1/4 c. mozzarella cheese, diced
    and divided

In a large serving bowl, combine beans, corn, red peppers, salsa and vinegar. Add onion, reserving one tablespoon. Toss gently to blend well. Let stand 15 minutes to blend flavors. Just before serving, gently fold in half of cheese. Top with reserved onion and remaining cheese. For best flavor, serve within 30 minutes. Makes 6 servings.

Refrigerate salad greens in a plastic zipping bag, with a paper towel tucked in to absorb extra moisture. They'll stay crisp and fresh for up to 4 days.

Heath's Beans

Nannette Scarborough
Farmersville, LA

My stepson Heath loves to experiment and cook, and he made these for us on one visit. We fell in love with them. They are so good and so easy to make. So we named them Heath's Beans and I have cooked these from Texas to Pennsylvania! So, so so good.

1 lb. ground hot pork sausage
28-oz. can baked beans
16-oz. can pinto beans
14-1/2 oz. can diced tomatoes
    with hot green chiles

15-1/2 oz. can red kidney beans,
    drained and rinsed
1/2 c. light brown sugar, packed
3 T. honey

In a stockpot over medium heat, cook sausage until browned and crumbled. Partially drain, if desired. Add remaining ingredients and stir to mix well. Bring to a boil; reduce heat to medium-low. Simmer for about 30 minutes, stirring occasionally. Makes 8 servings.

Keep the pantry stocked with canned vegetables, creamy soups, rice mixes, pasta and other handy meal-makers. If you pick up 2 or 3 items whenever they're on sale, you'll have a full pantry in no time at all.

Easy-Peasy Salads & Sides

Simple Cheesy Broccoli

Kim Carwile
Brookneal, VA

I serve this as a quick side dish on weeknights. It's a good way to get picky kids and husbands to eat their vegetables! My mom made this many times during my childhood and it never gets old. Very simple but delicious. Add more cheese, if you like it super cheesy!

10-oz. pkg. frozen chopped
   broccoli
1 T. butter

pepper to taste
4 slices Cheddar cheese

Cook broccoli according to package directions; drain. Add butter; season with pepper. Top with sliced cheese. Cover and let stand for 2 to 3 minutes, until cheese is melted. Serves 2 to 3.

Easy Broccoli Bake

Crystal Shook
Catawba, NC

A great, easy side dish for any occasion.

2 10-oz. pkgs. frozen broccoli
   flowerets, thawed
15-1/2 oz. jar double Cheddar
   cheese sauce

1/4 c. Italian-seasoned dry
   bread crumbs
1 T. butter, melted

Combine broccoli and cheese sauce in a lightly greased 2-quart casserole dish; set aside. In a separate bowl, toss bread crumbs with melted butter; spread evenly over broccoli mixture. Bake, uncovered, at 350 degrees for 20 minutes, or until broccoli is tender and bread crumbs are toasted. Serves 6 to 8.

A flavorful drizzle for steamed veggies! Simmer 1/2 cup balsamic vinegar over medium-low heat, stirring often, until thickened. So simple and scrumptious.

California-Blend Vegetable Casserole

Sherry Sheehan
Evensville, TN

This is a twist on the classic green bean casserole I love to make for holidays and special occasions. I enjoy trying it different ways, depending on what ingredients I have on hand. Sometimes I substitute regular mixed vegetables for California-blend mix. Try it with different cheeses like mozzarella and Pepper Jack, too.

16-oz. pkg. frozen California-
blend vegetables, thawed
10-3/4 oz. can cream of
mushroom or celery soup
1/3 c. sour cream
1/4 t. pepper
1 c. shredded Swiss cheese,
divided
1.3-oz. can French fried onions,
divided

Combine all ingredients in a lightly greased one-quart casserole dish, reserving 1/2 cup shredded cheese and 1/2 can onions. Bake, uncovered, at 350 degrees for 30 minutes. Sprinkle with reserved cheese and onions; return to oven. Bake another 5 minutes, or until cheese is melted. Makes 6 servings.

Frozen veggie spirals are a great time-saver and a healthy substitute for noodles and pasta. Look for spiralized zucchini, butternut and spaghetti squash in the freezer department. Simply heat and serve!

Easy-Peasy Salads & Sides

Cornbread Zucchini Bake

Marian Forck
Chamois, MO

A tasty recipe from Ev, my good neighbor and friend.
We love sharing our recipes and veggies! Peel the zucchini
before grating or not, as you like.

8-1/2 oz. pkg. corn muffin mix
1/2 c. butter, melted
4 eggs, beaten

3 c. zucchini, grated
8-oz. pkg. shredded Cheddar
cheese

In a large bowl, stir together dry muffin mix, melted butter and eggs.
Fold in zucchini and cheese. Spoon evenly into a lightly greased
13"x9" baking pan. Bake, uncovered, at 400 degrees for 25 minutes.
Makes 8 servings.

Make a chopped salad in seconds...no cutting board needed!
Add all the salad fixings except dressing to a big bowl,
then roll a pizza cutter back & forth over them. Drizzle
with dressing and enjoy your salad.

Easy-Peasy Slaw Salad

Marsha Baker
Pioneer, OH

A quick, luscious dish that gets a lot of attention because of simple ingredients. It's colorful and crunchy too.

16-oz. pkg frozen peas, thawed
14-oz. pkg. shredded
   coleslaw mix

4 to 5 green onions, chopped
1 c. poppy seed salad dressing
1 c. honey-roasted peanuts

Combine peas, coleslaw mix and onions in a large bowl; toss to mix. Stir in salad dressing; stir in peanuts or sprinkle on top. May serve immediately, or cover and refrigerate until ready to serve, adding peanuts at serving time. Serves 10.

Jazz up a packaged wild rice mix! Sauté a cup of chopped mushrooms, onion and celery in butter until tender, then add rice mix and prepare as usual.

Easy-Peasy Salads & Sides

Corn & Pepper Salad

Karen Chandler
Madison Heights, MI

This is a very quick & easy side dish. If you have leftover corn on the cob, it's delicious in this salad! You'll need about three cups.

1/4 c. white wine vinegar
2 T. olive oil
2 t. sugar
1/4 t. salt
1/4 t. pepper

16-oz. pkg. frozen corn, thawed
1-1/2 c. assorted red, orange and
green peppers, chopped
1/3 c. green onions, sliced

In a large serving bowl, whisk together vinegar, olive oil, sugar, salt and pepper. Stir in remaining ingredients. Cover and refrigerate until ready to serve. Makes 6 servings.

Sour Cream Rice

Ann Farris
Biscoe, AR

We are rice farmers, so rice is on our table often. This recipe is easy and oh-so good.

14-oz. can chicken broth
1 c. long-cooking jasmine rice,
uncooked
1 c. shredded Monterey Jack
cheese, divided

1 c. sour cream
15-1/4 oz. can corn, drained
4-oz. can chopped green chiles
1/4 t. salt

In a large saucepan over medium heat, bring chicken broth and rice to a boil. Cover and reduce heat to low. Simmer for 20 minutes, or until broth is absorbed and rice is tender. Stir in 1/2 cup cheese and remaining ingredients. Transfer mixture to a greased 8"x8" baking pan; top with remaining cheese. Bake, uncovered, at 350 degrees for 30 minutes, or until bubbly and golden. Serves 6 to 8.

Grandma's Best
RECIPES

Garlic Butter Vegetables

Coonstance Lewis
Florence, AL

This is a simple way to dress up frozen vegetables. It works well with a single frozen veggie like corn, green beans or peas, too.

16-oz. pkg. frozen mixed
   vegetables
1 c. low-sodium chicken broth
2 T. butter

1 t. garlic, minced
1 T. fresh parsley, chopped
salt and coarse pepper to taste
2 T. grated Parmesan cheese

Cook frozen vegetables in chicken broth according to package directions; drain. Stir in butter and garlic. Simmer for several minutes, stirring often, until butter coats vegetables. Remove from heat; add parsley, salt and pepper. Sprinkle with cheese and serve. Makes 4 to 6 servings.

Mediterranean Green Beans

Mia Rossi
Charlotte, NC

A fresh-tasting chilled side you can mix up in minutes.

14-1/2 oz. can cut green beans,
   drained
1/2 c. crumbled feta cheese
1/4 c. sun-dried tomatoes,
   drained and chopped

3 T. chopped black olives,
   drained
1/2 c. Greek vinaigrette
   salad dressing

In a large serving bowl, combine all ingredients except salad dressing; mix gently. Drizzle with salad dressing; stir to mix evenly. Cover and refrigerate for 2 to 3 hours, until chilled. Makes 6 servings.

Easy-Peasy Salads & Sides

Broccoli & Brown Rice Casserole

Nola Coons
Gooseberry Patch

Old-fashioned comfort food goodness...easy to make, easy to enjoy!

1 c. instant brown rice, uncooked
1 T. butter
10-oz. pkg. frozen chopped
   broccoli, thawed
1/2 c. onion, chopped
1/2 c. celery, chopped

10-3/4 oz. can cream of
   mushroom soup
1 c. pasteurized process cheese,
   diced
5-oz. can evaporated milk

Prepare rice according to package directions; set aside. Meanwhile, melt butter in a skillet over medium heat; sauté broccoli, onion and celery for 3 to 5 minutes. Stir in mushroom soup, cheese and milk; cook and stir until smooth. Add cooked rice; stir until blended. Spread evenly in a greased 8"x8" baking pan. Bake, uncovered, at 325 degrees for 25 to 30 minutes, until hot and bubbly. Makes 6 to 8 servings.

A great bridal shower gift for a new bride! Fill a basket with herbs, spices and seasoning mixes...tuck in copies of your favorite recipes. Wrap in colored cellophane and add a big bow. Done in one trip around the supermarket, and sure to be appreciated.

Southwest Hashbrown Casserole

Janice Curtis
Yucaipa, CA

A great side dish recipe...any leftovers are good with breakfast.

2 c. frozen diced hashbrowns, thawed
1/2 c. onion, diced
10-3/4 oz. can cream of onion soup
1/2 c. sour cream
1/4 c. fresh cilantro, chopped
1 c. shredded Pepper Jack cheese
1/2 c. shredded Cheddar cheese

Combine all ingredients in a large bowl. Mix well and spread in a greased 13"x9" baking pan. Bake, uncovered, at 350 degrees for 35 to 40 minutes, until bubbly and golden. Makes 4 to 6 servings.

Quick Refried Beans

Teresa Grimsley
Alamosa, CO

When you don't have time to fix refried beans from scratch, this is quick & easy...and so much better than canned refried beans! You can also use black beans or whatever kind of beans suits your taste.

1 onion, diced
1 to 2 t. oil
2 16-oz. cans pinto beans, one can drained
1 t. chili powder
1 t. garlic powder
1/2 t. paprika
1/8 t. ground cumin
1 jalapeño pepper, diced
1 T. lime juice
chopped parsley to taste
Optional: shredded Cheddar cheese, additional chopped parsley

In a skillet over medium heat, sauté onion in oil until soft. Add beans with liquid from one can and remaining ingredients; stir well. Simmer for about 20 minutes, stirring occasionally. With an immersion blender, process mixture in pan to desired consistency. Garnish as desired. Serves 6.

Easy-Peasy Salads & Sides

Stacie's Company Potatoes

Barbara Imler
Noblesville, IN

My oldest daughter served this dish one Thanksgiving and everyone raved about it. You would never guess it's made with instant potatoes! It solves the need for make-ahead mashed potatoes.

4 c. instant mashed potatoes, uncooked
8-oz. pkg. cream cheese, softened
1 c. sour cream
1 t. onion salt
1 t. garlic salt
Garnish: paprika

Prepare instant potatoes according to package directions for 12 servings; set aside. In a large bowl, beat together cream cheese and sour cream with an electric mixer on medium speed. Stir in prepared potatoes and salts. Spread evenly in a buttered 13"x9" baking pan; sprinkle with paprika. Bake, uncovered, at 375 degrees for 35 to 45 minutes, until heated through. Serves 10 to 12.

Caramelized onions are full of flavor and easy to make. Add 1/2 cup butter and 6 to 8 sliced onions to a slow cooker. Cover and cook on low setting for 10 to 12 hours, stirring once or twice. Spoon onions over meat dishes, or stir into casseroles to add savory flavor.

Brocco-Cauli Stuffing Casserole

Constance Bockstoce
Dallas, GA

Trying to get more vegetables into our diet, I went to a favorite recipe and tweaked it to include two healthy vegetables. It seemed to do the trick!

12-oz. pkg. frozen brocoli flowerets
5-1/4 oz. pkg. cornbread stuffing mix
1-1/4 c. hot water
1/4 c. butter, melted

10-3/4 oz. can cream of broccoli soup
12-oz. pkg. frozen cauliflower rice
8-oz. pkg. shredded Cheddar cheese

Place frozen broccoli in a covered microwave-safe bowl. Microwave for 5 to 6 minutes; drain. Meanwhile, combine stuffing mix, hot water and melted butter in a large bowl; mix well. Add broccoli soup and cooked broccoli; mix well and set aside. Add frozen cauliflower rice to same bowl used for broccoli; cover and microwave for 5 to 6 minutes. Add cheese and cooked cauliflower rice to stuffing mixture; mix well. Transfer evenly to a buttered 3-quart casserole dish, lightly pressing down. Bake, uncovered, at 350 degrees for about 45 minutes, until bubbly and golden. Makes 6 servings.

It's not how much we have, but how much we enjoy, that makes happiness.
–Charles Haddon-Spurgeon

Easy-Peasy Salads & Sides

Tasha's Caesar Tortellini Salad

Tasha Petenzi
Goodlettsville, TN

I make lots of different pasta salads, but this one is very different from the rest! So easy and delicious. It makes a fantastic side dish with grilled meats, or a great complement to a sandwich for lunch.

19-oz. pkg. frozen cheese
   tortellini, uncooked
8-oz. bottle Caesar salad dressing
1 cucumber, chopped
1 green pepper, chopped
Optional: 1/4 c. grated Parmesan
   cheese

Cook tortellini according to package directions; drain and rinse with cold water. In a large bowl, combine tortellini, salad dressing, cucumber and green pepper; toss to mix well. Cover and refrigerate at least one hour. Top with Parmesan cheese, if desired. Serves 6.

Tammy's Quick BLT Salad

Carolyn Deckard
Bedford, IN

My daughter Tammy treats us to this quick and flavorful pasta salad at family gatherings.

7-1/2 oz. pkg. ranch & bacon
   pasta salad mix, uncooked
1/2 c. mayonnaise
3 c. lettuce, finely shredded
1 ripe tomato, coarsely chopped

Cook pasta from salad mix according to package directions; drain and rinse with cold water. Meanwhile, in a large bowl, stir together pasta seasoning mix and mayonnaise. Add cooked pasta, lettuce and tomato; stir together until well blended. Serve immediately. Makes 6 servings.

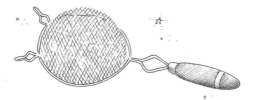

Summer Pea Salad

Diana Krol
Hutchinson, KS

This is the perfect side dish for your picnic or family barbecue. You don't even need to cook the peas!

1/2 c. sour cream
1/3 c. mayonnaise
1 T. sugar
2 t. vinegar
salt and pepper to taste

4 c. frozen peas
6 slices bacon, crisply cooked
    and diced
1/2 c. red onion, chopped
1/2 c. shredded Cheddar cheese

In a large serving bowl, whisk together sour cream, mayonnaise, sugar, vinegar and seasonings. Fold in remaining ingredients. Cover and chill for several hours. Serve chilled. Makes 6 to 8 servings.

Jazz up creamy bottled salad dressings...stir in a dollop of Greek yogurt or sour cream. Cheese-based dressings benefit from a little extra crumbled feta or blue cheese.

Easy-Peasy Salads & Sides

Marinated Vegetables

Vickie
Gooseberry Patch

*So, so easy and picnic-perfect! Sometimes I'll add some
black olives...it's scrumptious with Caesar salad dressing too.*

1-1/2 c. broccoli flowerets
1-1/2 c. cauliflower flowerets
1 green pepper, cut into
   1-inch pieces
1 cucumber, peeled, seeded
   and chopped

1 carrot, peeled and coarsely
   chopped
1/4 to 1/2 c. zesty Italian
   salad dressing

Bring a large pot of salted water to a rolling boil over high heat. Add
broccoli and cauliflower; boil for one minute. Drain and rinse vegetables;
transfer to a large serving bowl. Add remaining ingredients; toss to mix
well. Cover and chill until serving time. Makes 6 to 8 servings.

Turn yesterday's leftover mashed potatoes into crispy potato
pancakes! Stir an egg yolk and a little minced onion into 2 cups
cold potatoes. Form into patties, dust with a little flour and
pan-fry in oil or butter until golden.

SHORTCUTS TO
Grandma's Best
RECIPES

Creamy Carrots & Onions

Lynda Hart
Bluffdale, UT

I love to pick up fresh carrots and onions at the farmers' market. This is a tasty way to enjoy them.

6 to 8 carrots, peeled and sliced
1-1/2 c. onions, sliced
10-3/4 oz. can cream of
    chicken soup

2 T. butter
1 t. salt
1/2 t. pepper
Optional: chopped fresh parsley

In a large saucepan, cover carrots and onions with water. Bring to a boil; simmer for 10 minutes, or until tender. Drain, reserving 1/2 cup cooking water; return to pan. Add chicken soup, reserved cooking water, butter, salt and pepper; stir until smooth. Heat through, stirring occasionally. Garnish with parsley, if desired. Serves 6.

Sautéed Asparagus & Bacon

Nancy Wise
Little Rock, AR

So simple, yet delicious.

1 lb. asparagus, trimmed
6 slices bacon, cut into
    1-inch pieces

salt and pepper to taste
juice of 1/2 lemon

Cut asparagus into one-inch pieces; set aside. Cook bacon in a skillet over medium heat until crisp. Remove bacon to paper towels, reserving drippings in pan. Add asparagus to skillet. Cook for 5 to 6 minutes, until tender-crisp. Return bacon to skillet; season with salt and pepper. Squeeze lemon juice over asparagus; toss and serve. Makes 4 servings.

Fresh fruits and veggies are delicious partners in many recipes, but keep them separated in the fridge. Most fruits will cause lettuce and other greens to spoil more quickly.

Easy-Peasy Salads & Sides

Cheesy Green Beans & Potatoes
Alice Joy Randall
Nacogdoches, TX

As a young bride, a potato casserole was my first original recipe. Later, I began making a similar recipe with green beans. Only recently, many years later, I decided to combine the two using canned diced potatoes This dish goes well with any kind of meat and is easily doubled.

15-oz. can diced potatoes,
    drained
14-1/2 oz. can cut green
    beans, drained
10-3/4 oz. can cream of
    mushroom soup

1/2 c. milk
pepper to taste
2 slices American cheese,
    torn into pieces

Combine potatoes and green beans in a lightly greased 2-quart casserole dish; set aside. Whisk together mushroom soup and milk in a bowl; add to potato mixture and mix gently. Season with pepper Bake, uncovered, at 350 degrees for 30 minutes. Remove from oven; top with cheese. Let stand until cheese melts; gently stir cheese into casserole. Season with additional pepper and serve. Serves 4 to 6.

Check out handy salad kits in the produce aisle. Available in varieties like Asian cabbage and Buffalo ranch, they offer toss & serve ease. Make them your own by adding chopped chicken or veggies.

Broccoli Slaw Salad

Patricia Weigert
Plymouth, WI

I use this recipe whenever I need a dish to take to an outdoor gathering. A lot of variations can be made on this salad. Instead of dried cranberries, you can add diced apples or pineapple, grapes, pine nuts and walnuts, to name a few. It's easily doubled.

16-oz. pkg. shredded
   broccoli slaw
3/4 c. dried cranberries
Optional: 1/4 c. red onion, diced

3/4 c. poppy seed salad dressing
salt and pepper to taste
3/4 c. sliced almonds

In a large salad bowl, combine broccoli slaw, cranberries and onion, if using. Mix in salad dressing; season with salt and pepper. Cover and chill for one hour. Just before serving, mix again, adding additional dressing if needed. Fold in almonds and serve. Makes 6 servings.

Pick up a vintage divided serving dish...just right for serving up
a choice of sides without crowding the table.

Easy-Peasy Salads & Sides

Family-Favorite Caesar Salad

Sarah Cameron
Fort Belvoir, VA

Goes together in a snap...just watch this salad disappear!

9-oz. pkg. Romaine lettuce
   hearts
1/2 to 1 c. shredded Parmesan
   cheese

1/2 c. salad croutons
cracked pepper to taste
1/2 c. favorite Caesar salad
   dressing

Thinly slice lettuce hearts; trim off stalks. Add lettuce to a large salad bowl; top with desired amounts of Parmesan cheese, croutons and pepper. Use salad tongs to mix everything together. Add salad dressing; mix to coat well and serve. Makes 4 servings.

Make homemade croutons for soups and salads! Cube day-old bread, toss with olive oil and sprinkle with seasonings. Bake at 350 degrees for just a few minutes, until crisp. Store in tightly closed jars in the fridge. Try a batch of herb or Parmesan cheese-flavored!

Southwest Cauliflower Rice Salad

Teresa Eller
Kansas City, KS

Our son-in-law doesn't care for mayonnaise, so I made this salad to go along with our barbecue burgers. He loved it! As a variation, I have used pasta instead of cauliflower rice...either way is good.

10-oz. pkg. frozen
    cauliflower rice
10-oz. pkg. frozen corn
15-1/2 oz. can black beans
3/4 c. onion, chopped

16-oz. jar favorite salsa
1 c. ranch salad dressing
8 slices Pepper Jack cheese,
    stacked and cut into chunks

Separately cook cauliflower and corn according to package directions. Drain; allow to cool. Transfer cauliflower and corn to a large salad bowl; add beans with liquid and remaining ingredients. Toss to mix well; cover and chill until serving time. Makes 6 to 8 servings.

Ripe red tomatoes and sweet onions from the farmers' market are such a treat...serve them simply, with just a dash of oil & vinegar and a sprinkle of basil.

Easy-Peasy Salads & Sides

Mexicali Beans

Deeana Cole
Leesburg, FL

I came up with this dish, using some ingredients I had on hand...everyone loved it!

15-1/2 oz. can chili beans
15-1/2 oz. can black beans,
  drained and rinsed
15-1/4 oz. can corn, drained

1 green pepper, finely diced
1/2 red onion, finely diced
salt to taste

In a large saucepan, combine undrained chili beans and remaining ingredients. Cook over medium heat, stirring often, until well mixed and heated through. Reduce heat to medium-low; simmer until green pepper and onion are tender. Makes 6 to 8 servings.

Simple Baked Beans

Patricia Hall
Hobart, IN

A delicious recipe I've made for my family for many years.

1/2 lb. bacon, chopped
1 yellow onion, chopped
1 c. brown sugar, packed

1 c. catsup
32-oz. jar Great Northern beans,
  drained

In a skillet over medium heat, cook bacon with onion until crisp; drain. Combine brown sugar and catsup in a bowl; add to bacon mixture in skillet along with drained beans. Simmer over low heat for 20 to 25 minutes, stirring occasionally. Makes 6 servings.

If brown sugar has hardened in the package, simply grate the amount needed in a recipe...a quick fix!

Easy Mushroom Pilaf

Sarah Oravecz
Gooseberry Patch

This easy side dish cooks up in no time! Stir in some green peas, if you like.

2 T. butter
1/4 c. onion, chopped
1 c. long-cooking rice, uncooked
2 c. chicken broth

4-oz. can sliced mushrooms, drained
1/4 t. salt
pepper to taste

Melt butter in a saucepan over medium heat; add onion. Cook until tender, stirring occasionally. Stir in uncooked rice; cook for 5 minutes, stirring often. Stir in chicken broth, mushrooms and salt; bring to a boil. Reduce heat to low; cover and simmer for 15 to 18 minutes. Remove from heat. Let stand, covered, for about 5 minutes, until rice is tender. Season with pepper and serve. Makes 4 servings.

A real kitchen time-saver! A silicon hot pad can function as trivet, potholder, anti-slip pad for mixing bowls, jar opener and garlic peeler. Pick up several in your favorite colors.

Easy-Peasy Salads & Sides

Quick Rice Pilaf with Veggies

Jen Thomas
Santa Rosa, CA

We enjoy this easy recipe with grilled chicken or fish.

14-1/2 oz. can chicken broth
2 c. frozen mixed stir-fry
    vegetables

1-1/4 t. onion powder
1-3/4 c. instant rice, uncooked
2 T. butter

In a saucepan over medium heat, bring chicken broth to a boil. Add frozen vegetables and onion powder. Simmer for 5 minutes, or until vegetables are tender. Stir in uncooked rice; remove from heat. Cover and let sit 5 minutes. Stir in butter and serve. Serves 6.

Classic Fried Rice

Emma Brown
Saskatchewan, Canada

An easy side dish, or add a can of shredded chicken and serve as a simple main dish.

1 T. oil
2 c. instant rice, uncooked
2 eggs, lightly beaten

1 c. chicken broth
1 c. frozen mixed vegetables
3 T. soy sauce

Heat oil in a large skillet or wok over medium heat. Add uncooked rice and cook for about 3 minutes, until lightly golden. Add eggs; cook and stir until set. Add chicken broth, frozen vegetables and soy sauce; bring to a boil. Remove from heat; cover and let stand for 5 minutes, or until vegetables are tender. Makes 4 servings.

Better than a feast elsewhere is a meal at home of tea and rice.
-Japanese proverb

Grandma's Best

German Potato Casserole

Carol Lytle
Columbus, OH

*Creamy and delicious, with crunchy toppings...a nice change
from our usual hashbrown casserole recipe.*

10-3/4 oz. can cream of
    potato soup
1-1/2 c. sour cream
3 T. white vinegar
32-oz. pkg. frozen diced
    hashbrowns, thawed

8-oz. pkg. shredded Swiss cheese
8 slices bacon, crisply cooked,
    crumbled and divided
6 green onions, sliced and
    divided
2 c. French fried onions

In a large bowl, whisk together potato soup, sour cream and vinegar
until well blended. Add hashbrowns, cheese, 1/4 cup crumbled bacon
and 1/2 cup green onions; mix lightly. Spoon evenly into a greased
13"x9" baking pan. Bake, uncovered, at 350 degrees for about
50 minutes, until hot and bubbly; top with French fried onions after
20 minutes. Just before serving, sprinkle with remaining bacon and
onions. Makes 8 to 10 servings.

Shredded coleslaw mix eliminates the time you'd normally take
to rinse and chop cabbage. Toss with bottled coleslaw dressing
for a fresh side in a jiffy...add it to soups and casseroles
that call for chopped cabbage.

Easy-Peasy Salads & Sides

Maple-Glazed Sweet Potatoes

Delores Lakes
Mansfield, OH

Sweet potatoes are so nutritious...and delicious! At our Christmas holiday dinners, they were always served alongside the mashed potatoes. Just seeing them served in a pretty bowl with their deep orange color makes me happy!

1/2 c. orange juice
1 T. cornstarch
3 T. butter
1/2 c. pure maple syrup

1 t. orange zest
2 15-3/4 oz. cans cut sweet
    potatoes, drained

In a small bowl, combine orange juice and cornstarch; stir well and set aside. Melt butter in a large skillet over medium heat. Add orange juice mixture, maple syrup and orange zest. Cook and stir for several minutes, until thickened and clear. Add sweet potatoes; stir to coat well and heat through. Makes 6 to 8 servings.

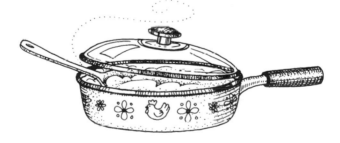

All we need to make us really happy is something
to be enthusiastic about.
–Charles Kingsley

Slow-Cooker Glazed Green Beans

Pam Lunn
Pensacola, FL

This easy recipe is one of my favorites, and it is usually on my holiday menu. It is so easy to make, and goes well with beef, pork, turkey or chicken. Be sure to use teriyaki baste & glaze sauce, not marinade. I hope your family enjoys it as much as mine does!

28-oz. pkg frozen cut
  green beans
2.8-oz. jar real bacon bits
1/2 c. teriyaki baste &
  glaze sauce

1/2 c. yellow onion, minced
1/4 c. low-sodium chicken broth
1 t. garlic, minced
pepper to taste

Spray a 4-quart slow cooker with non-stick vegetable spray. Add all ingredients to slow cooker; stir until thoroughly combined. Cover and cook on high setting for 3 to 4 hours, or on low setting for 6 to 8 hours. Keeps well set on low after cooking. Makes 10 to 12 servings.

Boxed stuffing mixes are a tasty, quick side for baked chicken and pork. Make them your own by browning the butter first, and use chicken or veggie broth instead of water. You can even use apple juice and add some chopped dried fruit for a sweet stuffing.

Easy-Peasy Salads & Sides

Sweet-and-Sour Beets

Sandy Ward
Anderson, IN

I love vegetables and always try to encourage others to taste everything. You don't know unless you try...you may even like it! If you're unable to find diced beets, get sliced beets and dice them.

15-oz. can diced beets	1 T. sugar
1 t. butter	1 T. vinegar
2 T. cornstarch	

Add beets with liquid to a saucepan; liquid should nearly cover beets. Hear through over medium heat; add butter. Blend cornstarch, sugar and vinegar in a cup; add to beets. Cook until thickened, stirring often. If mixture becomes too thick, add a small amount of water. Makes 4 servings.

Orange Carrots

Kathy Courington
Canton, GA

A quick & easy side to go with whatever meat you're serving.

1 lb. baby carrots, thinly sliced	1 T. orange zest
1/4 c. butter	1 t. sugar

Combine all ingredients in a buttered one-quart microwave-safe casserole dish. Cover and microwave on high for 4 to 6 minutes, until carrots are tender, stirring after half the time. Stir again and serve. Makes 6 servings.

One tablespoon of a chopped fresh herb equals one teaspoon of the dried variety...simple to substitute!

Wild Rice Vegetable Salad

Karen Antonides
Gahanna, OH

*This vegetable-packed salad is great any time of year.
From picnics and cookouts to holiday tables, it is a
welcome addition and always disappears quickly.*

6-oz. pkg. long grain & wild rice,
　uncooked
10-oz. pkg. frozen peas
6-1/2 oz. jar marinated artichoke
　hearts, drained
6-oz. can sliced black olives,
　drained

1 pt. grape tomatoes, halved
3 green onions, sliced
1/2 to 1 bunch fresh parsley,
　finely chopped

Cook rice according to package directions; transfer to a large salad bowl
and set aside to cool. Meanwhile, bring a saucepan of water to a boil
over medium heat. Add frozen peas and cook for 2 minutes; drain and
cool. Add peas and remaining ingredients to rice in bowl. Drizzle with
Dressing; toss to coat well. Cover and refrigerate until ready to serve.
Makes 8 servings.

Dressing:

1/2 c. white balsamic vinegar
1/4 c. canola oil

1/4 c. sugar

Whisk together all ingredients until well blended.

Save the liquid from jars of marinated artichokes. It's great
for adding zest to bland salad dressings or a pot of cooked beans.

Easy-Peasy Salads & Sides

Fat Tony's Pasta Salad

Julie Perkins
Anderson, IN

This is great at potlucks. There's a little Italian in everyone!

1-1/2 c. medium pasta shells,
  uncooked
3-1/2 oz. pkg. sliced pepperoni,
  quartered

1 c. shredded mozzarella cheese
1 c. broccoli flowerets
1/2 c. Caesar salad dressing

Cook pasta according to package directions; drain and rinse with cold water. Meanwhile, combine pepperoni, cheese and broccoli in a large salad bowl. Add cooked pasta; drizzle with salad dressing and toss to combine. Cover and refrigerate until serving time. Makes 6 servings.

Jars of basil pesto sauce and sun-dried tomato pesto sauce are indispensable for busy days. Tossed with hot cooked pasta, or spread on baguette slices and topped with cheese, they're a flavorful side dish in just a few minutes.

Herb-Roasted Dijon Potatoes

Shelley Turner
Boise, ID

My whole family loves these savory potatoes, popped in the oven alongside roasted chicken or pork chops. Sometimes I'll use tiny whole mini potatoes just for fun.

2 lbs. redskin potatoes,
   cut into chunks
1/3 c. Dijon mustard

2 T. olive oil
1 clove garlic, minced
1/2 t. Italian seasoning

Spread potatoes in an oiled 13"x9" baking pan; set aside. Combine remaining ingredients in a small bowl; mix well and drizzle over potatoes. Toss to coat well. Bake, uncovered, at 425 degrees for 35 to 40 minutes, until potatoes are fork-tender. Makes 6 servings.

Ranch Mashed Potatoes

Connie Hilty
Pearland, TX

This is a great way to jazz up refrigerated or frozen mashed potatoes, or even leftovers.

1/2 c. sour cream
2 T. milk
1-oz. pkg. ranch salad
   dressing mix

2 c. mashed potatoes
Optional: shredded Cheddar
   cheese, bacon bits

In a large microwave-safe bowl, stir together sour cream and milk; blend in salad dressing mix. Add mashed potatoes; mix well. Microwave on high until heated through; top with cheese and bacon, if desired. Serves 4.

Keep a selection of rice pilaf mixes on hand for side dishes in a jiffy. You can even stir in some chopped cooked chicken for a quick main dish.

Easy-Peasy Salads & Sides

Pammy's Potatoes

Pamela Pierce
Lenoir, NC

*One day I was looking in the pantry for something quick & easy.
I spotted some cans of potatoes and cream of mushroom soup
sitting side by side. I combined them and decided it needed some
cheese...white American slices were perfect! Double or triple the
recipe with ease.*

10-3/4 oz. can cream of
  mushroom soup
2 T. water

4 slices white American cheese,
  torn into pieces
1 can sliced potatoes, drained

In a large saucepan, heat mushroom soup over medium heat until
warmed. Stir in water and cheese; heat through. Add potatoes and stir;
heat until hot and serve. Makes 4 servings.

Creamed Potatoes

Zoe Bennett
Columbia, SC

Old-fashioned comfort food, ready in a few minutes.

1/4 c. butter
1/4 c. all-purpose flour
2 c. milk

2 15-oz. cans sliced potatoes,
  drained
salt and pepper to taste

Melt butter in a saucepan over medium-high heat. Add flour; cook and
stir until blended. Mixture will be thick. Gradually stir in milk; cook and
stir until flour is dissolved and mixture is thickened and heated through.
Reduce heat to medium; stir in potatoes. Simmer until potatoes are
heated through, stirring occasionally, about 15 minutes. Season with
salt and pepper. Makes 6 servings.

A quick and yummy cheese sauce for veggies! Combine one cup
evaporated milk and 1/2 cup shredded cheese. Cook and
stir over low heat until smooth.

Orange Sherbet Salad

Joann Belovitch
Stratford, CT

We all love this scrumptious gelatin salad. Serve it as
a side dish or as a simple dessert.

6-oz. pkg. orange gelatin mix
2 c. boiling water
1 pt. orange sherbet, softened
11-oz. can mandarin oranges,
    drained

20-oz. can crushed pineapple,
    drained

In a large bowl, combine gelatin mix and boiling water. Stir for about 2 minutes, until gelatin is dissolved. Add sherbet; stir until melted. Fold in oranges and pineapple. Transfer mixture to an 8"x8" glass baking pan or a serving bowl. Cover and chill for several hours, until set. Makes 10 servings.

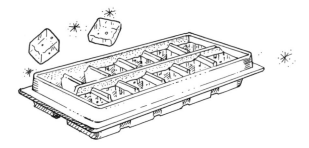

When draining canned fruit, freeze the juice in ice cube trays... handy for adding a little sweetness to marinades and dressings, or for chilling a favorite beverage.

Easy-Peasy Salads & Sides

Waldorf Salad

Laura Fuller
Fort Wayne, IN

An old-fashioned favorite...serve scooped onto ruffled lettuce, if desired.

3/4 c. mayonnaise
4 t. lemon juice
5 t. milk
1-1/2 c. celery, chopped

1/2 c. coarsely chopped walnuts
3 c. Red Delicious or Gala apples, cored and cubed

Mix mayonnaise, lemon juice and milk in a large salad bowl. Stir in celery, walnuts and apples. Cover and refrigerate until ready to serve. Makes 6 servings.

Easy Pineapple-Pistachio Salad

Wendy Bentley
Corvallis, OR

This refreshing and festive salad makes a wonderful side dish for special occasions. I make it often and share with friends and neighbors. Everyone loves it!

3.4-oz. pkg. instant pistachio
  pudding mix
20-oz. can crushed pineapple
10-oz. pkg. mini marshmallows

8-oz. container frozen whipped
  topping, thawed
Garnish: slivered almonds,
  halved maraschino cherries

In a large bowl, combine pudding mix and undrained pineapple; mix very well. Add marshmallows and mix thoroughly; fold in whipped topping. Transfer to a 9"x9" glass baking pan; cover and chill for one hour. Cut into squares; garnish as desired. Serves 10 to 12.

Show off the bright colors of a fruit salad...serve it in old-fashioned glass compotes.

Fluffy Fruit Salad

Carrie Kelderman
Pella, IA

A friend from church brought me this salad after I had my first baby. Since then, I have often brought this salad alongside a meal to bless others. Everyone loves it! Easily change up the flavor by using a different fruit...strawberry-banana gelatin with fresh strawberries is scrumptious too!

16-oz. container sour cream
16-oz. container frozen whipped
   topping, thawed

6-oz. pkg. raspberry gelatin mix
2 c. frozen raspberries, thawed
   and drained

In large bowl, combine sour cream, whipped topping and gelatin mix; stir until fluffy and well blended. Fold in berries; cover and chill until serving time. Makes 8 servings.

Fruity gelatin salads are yummy topped with a dollop of
creamy lemon mayonnaise. Stir 3 tablespoons each of
lemon juice, light cream and powdered sugar into
1/2 cup mayonnaise. Garnish with curls of lemon zest,
if you like.

Suppers in a Snap

Easy-Peasy Alfredo

Angela Pike
Russell Springs, KY

One night, I made this for my kids between marching band practice and theater rehearsal...it was a hit! It uses items I always keep in my pantry and fridge, yet tastes like one of our favorite restaurant dishes.

16-oz. pkg. thin spaghetti,
  uncooked
12-oz. pkg. frozen peas
2 T. butter
2-1/2 oz. pkg. fully cooked
  bacon, chopped

Optional: 8-oz. pkg. sliced
  mushrooms
2 15-oz. jars roasted garlic
  Alfredo sauce
salt and pepper to taste

Cook spaghetti according to package directions, adding frozen peas halfway through cooktime; drain. Meanwhile, melt butter in a skillet over medium heat; add bacon and mushrooms, if using. Sauté for several minutes. Add Alfredo sauce to mixture in skillet; stir well and heat through. To serve, divide spaghetti mixture among plates; top with sauce mixture and season with salt and pepper. Makes 6 to 8 servings.

Beginning a speedy supper? Check the recipe first, to make sure you have everything on hand before you begin...no last-minute trips to the store for a forgotten ingredient!

Suppers in a Snap

Grammie's Zesty Weeknight Chicken

Lisa Staib
Tumbling Shoals, AR

My mother, a cook of the 1940s to 70s, thought any "newfangled" bottle or packet dressing was a miracle shortcut, instead of pulling 15 ingredients from her kitchen shelves. This three-ingredient dish is great with any vegetable side...and a warm Parker House roll.

16-oz. bottle zesty Italian
   salad dressing
1 lb. boneless, skinless
   chicken tenders

2-oz. pkg. seasoned coating mix
   for chicken, divided

Pour salad dressing into an ungreased 13"x9" shallow baking pan. Add chicken tenders and stir to coat well. Sprinkle half of coating mix over chicken. Cover with aluminum foil. Bake at 350 degrees for 30 minutes. Uncover; turn chicken tenders over and sprinkle with remaining coating mix. Cover again and bake another 15 minutes. Remove foil and bake for 15 minutes more, or until chicken juices run clear when pierced. Serve chicken tenders with pan drippings. Makes 4 servings.

A full pantry makes it so easy to toss together all kinds of tasty meals in a jiffy. Stock the cupboard with cans of chicken, tuna, salmon and other canned meats along with packages of pasta and rice.

Cajun Sausage & Rice Skillet

Mori Green
Conroe, TX

My family is crazy about this dish! Turn it into a great jambalaya by adding one cup cooked chicken and/or shrimp, one cup diced tomatoes and one cup frozen okra.

3 T. olive oil
14-oz. pkg. smoked pork
   sausage, chopped
1/2 onion, chopped
1/2 green pepper, chopped

3 cloves garlic, pressed
2 c. water
5.6-oz. pkg. Spanish rice
   mix, uncooked

Heat oil in a skillet over medium heat; add sausage, onion, pepper and garlic. Cook until sausage is browned and vegetables are tender; drain. Stir in water and uncooked rice mix. Reduce heat to low; cover and simmer for 7 minutes, or until rice is tender. Remove from heat; let stand for 5 minutes before serving. Serves 4.

Keep an eye out for canned Italian cherry tomatoes! These sweet little morsels add rich flavor to soups and pasta sauces. Heap them on toasted baguette slices for a quick bruschetta, too.

Suppers in a Snap

Spinach Ravioli Lasagna

Annette Ceravolo
Hoover, AL

At our house, it's not Sunday unless you have pasta! We held true to this statement every Sunday while I was growing up, and I still have pasta every Sunday with my own family. When I have leftover sauce in the freezer, I'll thaw to use instead of buying it. It really saves time.

2 24-oz. jars marinara sauce, divided
3 13-oz. pkgs. frozen cheese or meat ravioli, uncooked
10-oz. pkg. frozen chopped spinach, thawed, squeezed dry and divided
8-oz. pkg. shredded mozzarella cheese, divided
1/2 c. grated Parmesan cheese

Spread a thin layer of marinara sauce in a lightly greased 13"x9" baking pan. Arrange ravioli over sauce in a single layer; top with half each of spinach, remaining sauce and mozzarella cheese. Repeat layers; top with Parmesan cheese. Cover with aluminum foil. Bake at 375 degrees for 35 minutes. Uncover and bake an additional 15 minutes, or until cheese is melted and ravioli is tender. Let stand for 5 minutes before serving. Serves 8.

Even a simple family supper can be memorable when it's thoughtfully served. Use the good china, set out cloth napkins and a vase of fresh flowers...after all, who's more special than your family?

Hamburger Patties & Country Gravy

Diane Bertosa
Brunswick Hills, OH

This is one of our most favorite recipes to make. It is so simple and yet delicious. Wonderful served with mashed potatoes topped with extra gravy...add a little more pepper, if you like an extra kick like my husband does!

1 lb. ground beef
1/2 c. dry bread crumbs
1 egg, beaten
1 T. Worcestershire sauce
1 t. seasoning salt

1 t. onion powder
1/2 t. garlic powder
1/2 t. pepper
2.6-oz. pkg. peppered country
   gravy mix

In a large bowl, combine all ingredients except gravy mix. Mix well and form into 4 patties. Add patties to a skillet over medium to medium-low heat. Cook for 15 to 20 minutes until well browned, turning every 5 minutes. Meanwhile, prepare gravy mix according to package directions. Serve patties topped with gravy. Serves 4.

The most indispensable ingredient of all good home cooking...
love, for those you are cooking for.
–Sophia Loren

Suppers in a Snap

Salsa Pork Loaf

*Regina Vining
Warwick, RI*

*My mom used to tear up slices of bread to add to her
meat loaf recipe. Packaged stuffing mix is easier...tastier, too!*

2 lbs. ground pork
6-oz. pkg. chicken-flavored
   stuffing mix
2 eggs, beaten

1/2 c. sour cream
1 green pepper, diced
4 slices bacon
1 c. favorite salsa, divided

In a large bowl, combine all ingredients except bacon and salsa; blend
well. Shape mixture into an oval loaf; place in a greased 13"x9" baking
pan. Top with bacon slices; spoon 1/2 cup salsa over loaf. Bake,
uncovered, at 350 degrees for 1-1/4 hours, or until cooked through.
Remove from oven; cover and let stand for 10 minutes. Slice loaf and
serve with remaining salsa, warmed. Makes 8 servings.

Hoosier Hamburger Casserole

*Angela Lengacher
Montgomery, IN*

*This dish was a favorite of my kids, Peyton and Luke.
They still loved it as they reached their teens...it's a winner!
I love that it's easy to make.*

7-1/4 oz. pkg. macaroni &
   cheese mix, uncooked
1 lb. ground beef
3/4 c. onion, chopped

10-3/4 oz. can cream of
   mushroom soup
4 to 5 slices American cheese

Prepare macaroni & cheese mix as package directs. Meanwhile, brown
beef and onion in a skillet over medium heat; drain well. Stir mushroom
soup into beef mixture; simmer for 2 to 3 minutes. Stir in macaroni &
cheese. Top with cheese slices; let stand until melted and serve.
Serves 6.

Enjoy sour cream to the last spoonful...after opening
a new container, stir in a teaspoon of white vinegar.

Crispy Chicken Tenders

Annette Ingram
Grand Rapids, MI

My kids beg for chicken nuggets from their favorite fast-food restaurant. But I have a trick up my sleeve...this recipe goes together quickly and they like it just as well!

8-1/2 oz. pkg. corn muffin mix
1 T. garlic herb seasoning
1 t. salt
1/2 t. pepper

2 lbs. boneless, skinless
   chicken tenders
1/2 c. oil

In a large plastic zipping bag, combine dry muffin mix and seasonings; mix well. Add chicken tenders to bag. Seal bag; shake to coat chicken thoroughly and set aside. Heat oil in a skillet over medium-high heat. Working in batches, carefully add chicken to hot oil. Cook, turning once, until chicken juices run clear when pierced. Drain chicken on paper towels and serve. Serves 6.

Serve chicken tenders with this easy, kid-friendly dipping sauce. Combine 1/3 cup catsup, 2 tablespoons maple syrup, 1/2 teaspoon Worcestershire sauce and 1/2 teaspoon soy sauce...yum!

Suppers in a Snap

Mac & Cheese Pizza

Lori Simmons
Princeville, IL

Easy and kid-friendly! For variety, try your favorite deluxe mac & cheese mix, like Cheddar broccoli or white Cheddar and herbs.

14-oz. pkg. deluxe macaroni &
   cheese mix, uncooked
1/2 lb. ground Italian pork
   sausage
13.8-oz. tube refrigerated
   pizza dough

1/2 c. green pepper
1 c. shredded mozzarella cheese
1/4 c. grated Parmesan cheese

Prepare macaroni & cheese mix as package directs. Meanwhile, brown sausage in a skillet over medium heat; drain. Unroll pizza dough and pat into a rectangle on a greased baking sheet, 1/4-inch thick. Bake at 400 degrees for 8 minutes. Remove from oven; spread macaroni & cheese over baked crust. Top with sausage, pepper and cheeses. Bake at 400 degrees for 10 to 12 minutes, until cheese is melted and edges of crust are golden. Cut into squares and serve. Makes 10 servings.

Set up a mini salad bar at dinner! Fill up a muffin tin with diced tomatoes, cucumbers and carrots, plus a choice of dressings. Family members can simply help themselves to toppings.

Slow-Cooker Asian Chicken & Fruit

Marian Forck
Chamois, MO

I love this recipe because it is so easy! While it is cooking in the slow cooker, you can relax and do other enjoyable things, like watching TV or reading. Add a steamed green vegetable and you have a good meal everyone will enjoy.

4 boneless, skinless chicken
    breasts
1/2 c. teriyaki sauce
1/2 c. soy sauce
11-oz. can mandarin oranges,
    drained

20-oz. can pineapple chunks,
    drained and half of juice
    reserved
1 T. garlic, minced
red pepper flakes to taste
Optional: cooked rice or noodles

Arrange chicken breasts in a lightly greased 4-quart slow cooker. Drizzle sauces over chicken. Add fruits and reserved pineapple juice; sprinkle with garlic and red pepper flakes. Cover and cook on high setting for 3 to 4 hours, until chicken is very tender. Shred chicken, if desired. Serve chicken over cooked rice or noodles, topped with fruit mixture from slow cooker. Makes 4 servings.

Chicken thighs are juicy and flavorful. Feel free to
substitute them in most recipes that call for chicken breasts.

Suppers in a Snap

Teriyaki Beef & Peppers

Tori Willis
Champaign, IL

*Easy and enjoyed by the whole family! Sometimes I'll add
a can of bamboo shoots instead of the water chestnuts.*

1 T. oil
1 lb. boneless beef sirloin steak,
   thinly sliced
14-oz. pkg. frozen stir-fry pepper
   blend
8-oz. can sliced water chestnuts,
   drained

14-1/2 oz. jar teriyaki stir-fry
   sauce & marinade
cooked lo mein noodles or
   linguine pasta

Heat oil in a large skillet or wok over high heat; add beef strips. Cook
and stir for about 5 minutes, until beef is browned on all sides. Remove
beef from wok; set aside. Add frozen peppers; cook for 5 minutes, or
until crisp-tender. Return beef to skillet; add water chestnuts and stir-fry
sauce. Simmer for one to 2 minutes, until heated through. Serve beef
mixture ladled over cooked noodles. Makes 5 servings.

If your favorite non-stick skillet is sticky, fill it with one cup water,
1/2 cup vinegar and 2 tablespoons baking soda. Bring to a boil for
a few minutes. Rinse well with hot water and wipe clean...
no more stickiness!

Very Good Casserole

Eugenia Taylor
Stroudsburg, PA

My kids always ask for this on cold Sunday afternoons...it's their favorite and always a hit with the family. The recipe was given to me by my friend years ago and has become a go-to ever since.

8-oz. pkg. wide egg noodles,
  uncooked
1 lb. ground beef
1 onion, chopped
3 8-oz. cans tomato sauce

3-oz. pkg. cream cheese, cubed
8-oz. container sour cream
1 to 2 c. shredded mozzarella
  cheese

Cook noodles according to package directions, until nearly tender; drain. Meanwhile, cook beef in a skillet over medium heat until nearly browned. Add onion and cook until done; drain. Stir in tomato sauce; simmer for several minutes, until well blended. Add cream cheese and stir until melted. Add sour cream and cooked noodles; mix well. Transfer mixture to a buttered 3-quart casserole dish; top with desired amount of mozzarella cheese. Bake, uncovered, at 350 degrees for about 30 minutes, until bubbly and cheese is melted. Serves 6.

On Friday nights, turn leftovers into a buffet-style meal. Set out casserole portions in pretty dishes, toss veggies into a salad and add a basket of warm rolls. Arrange everything on a counter... everyone is sure to come looking for their favorites!

Suppers in a Snap

Judi's One-Dish Meal

Judi Lance
Payson, AZ

One day I didn't have much planned for dinner, so I started looking in the refrigerator and pantry. These items are what I found. The flavors went together so well...it's very delicious! Serve with warm biscuits or garlic bread.

1 to 1-1/2 lbs. ground beef
1/2 c. onion, chopped
1 green pepper, chopped
1 t. garlic powder

5-oz. pkg. seasoned yellow rice, uncooked
salt and pepper to taste

In a skillet over medium heat, cook beef with onion, green pepper and garlic powder; drain. Meanwhile, cook rice according to package directions, until tender. Add beef mixture to rice; stir well. Season with salt and pepper and serve. Makes 4 servings.

Boil-in-bag rice cooks up in no time at all...no measuring, no watching. Just drop the bag into a saucepan of boiling water and set the timer! Even quicker...heat & eat rice packages. Just microwave and serve.

Creamy Mushroom Chicken & Rice

Jenessa Yauch
McKeesport, PA

My mother always made this recipe when I was growing up. It is so simple to fix and warms your soul. I could eat the delicious mushroom sauce and rice alone until my tummy is full...I recommend you give it a try!

4 to 5 boneless, skinless chicken
    breasts
salt and pepper to taste
2 T. olive oil
2 10-3/4 oz. cans cream of
    mushroom soup

2 c. water
2 cubes chicken bouillon
2 c. instant rice, uncooked
2 c. boiling water

Season chicken breasts with salt and pepper. Heat oil in a deep skillet over medium heat. Add chicken and brown on both sides; drain. Meanwhile, whisk together mushroom soup and water in a large bowl. Spoon over chicken in skillet; add bouillon cubes. Bring to a boil; stir and reduce heat to medium-low. Cover and simmer for about one hour, until chicken is cooked through. Meanwhile, combine rice and boiling water. Cover and let stand for 5 minutes; fluff with a fork. Serve chicken with rice, topped with mushroom sauce from skillet. Makes 4 to 5 servings.

Add a little butter to the oil when sautéing meats and vegetables.
It adds delicious flavor and helps foods cook up golden.

Suppers in a Snap

Quick Shepherd's Pie

Michelle West
Garland, TX

*My mom used to make this dish for my brother and me, growing up.
The barbecue sauce was Mom's own twist on shepherd's pie. It is
comfort food at its best. Serve with a tossed salad and hot rolls.*

1 lb. ground beef or turkey
3/4 c. yellow onion, diced
Optional: 2 to 3 t. oil
2 18.8-oz. cans chunky
   vegetable soup, divided

1/4 c. favorite barbecue sauce
24-oz. container refrigerated
   mashed potatoes
Optional: butter or shredded
   cheese

In a skillet over medium heat, brown beef or turkey with onion,
adding oil if needed. Drain; add one can vegetable soup to skillet. Drain
remaining can of soup; add to skillet along with barbecue sauce. Mix
well. Spread mixture evenly in a 13"x9" baking pan coated with non-
stick vegetable spray. Top with mashed potatoes and spread evenly.
If desired, top potatoes with pats of butter or shredded cheese. Bake,
uncovered, at 350 degrees for 30 minutes. Remove from oven; let stand
for 10 minutes and serve. Makes 4 to 6 servings.

Here's another tasty shortcut for Shepherd's Pie! Instead of
mashed potatoes, top with mini potato puffs and a sprinkle of
shredded cheese. Bake until crisp and golden...so good.

Batter-Top Sausage & Bean Casserole

*Donna Clement
Daphne, AL*

I used to love it when our kids were little and all the mothers would get together for play days. We'd share the dishes that we were planning to cook that week. This recipe was one of our favorites. I like to bake in a large cast-iron skillet and bring it right to the table to serve family-style.

1 lb. ground pork sausage
1 onion, chopped
1 to 2 cloves garlic, minced
2 14-1/2 oz. cans ranch-style
   beans
1-1/2 c. water

8-1/2 oz. pkg. corn muffin mix
1 egg, beaten
1/4 c. milk
8-oz. pkg. shredded Cheddar
   cheese

In a skillet over medium heat, brown sausage with onion and garlic; do not drain. Add undrained beans and water; stir well. Bring to a simmer. Transfer mixture to a lightly greased 4-quart casserole dish; set aside. In a bowl, combine dry corn muffin mix, egg and milk; mix well and pour batter over beef mixture. Bake, uncovered, at 400 degrees for 15 to 20 minutes, until cornbread is set and golden. Remove from oven; top with cheese. Return to oven for a few more minutes, until cheese melts. Makes 6 servings.

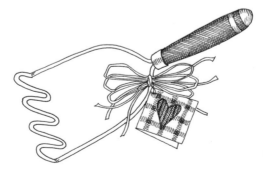

Crumble ground beef or sausage easily...mash it with
a potato masher as it browns in the skillet.

Suppers in a Snap

Ham & Swiss Noodle Bake

Janice Curtis
Yucaipa, CA

I first tried this recipe over twenty years ago,
and still love the flavor of everything in it.

16-oz. pkg. wide egg noodles,
   uncooked
2 T. butter
3/4 c. onion, chopped
3/4 c. green pepper, chopped

1-1/2 c. sour cream
2 10-3/4 oz. cans cream of
   mushroom soup
2 c. cooked ham, cubed
8-oz. pkg. shredded Swiss cheese

Cook noodles according to package directions; drain. Meanwhile, melt
butter in a saucepan over medium heat. Sauté onion and green pepper
until tender; remove from heat. Stir in sour cream, mushroom soup,
ham and cheese; fold in cooked noodles. Transfer to a greased 4-quart
casserole dish. Bake, uncovered, at 350 degrees for 35 to 40 minutes,
until hot and bubbly. Serves 4 to 6.

Stovetop Beef & Noodles

Linda Wagler
Montgomery, IN

A quick & easy one-dish meal your family will love.

1-1/2 c. narrow egg noodles,
   uncooked
1 lb. ground beef
1/4 c. onion, chopped
15-1/2 oz. can corn, drained

10-3/4 oz. can cream of
   mushroom soup
1-1/2 c. pasteurized process
   cheese, cubed
salt and pepper to taste

Cook noodles according to package directions; drain. Meanwhile, brown
beef with onion in a skillet over medium heat; drain. Stir in cooked
noodles and remaining ingredients. Cover and simmer over low heat
until hot, bubbly and cheese is melted. Serves 4.

Use a potato peeler to quickly cut thin curls of cheese for
garnishing soup, salad or pasta.

Quick Spanish Chicken & Rice

Shirley Howie
Foxboro, MA

This easy skillet meal can be on the table in about thirty minutes, making it a real winner! I like the convenience of using rotisserie chicken for this recipe...it also adds another layer of flavor.

2 T. butter
2 14-1/2 oz. cans diced
    tomatoes, drained
1/2 c. onion, finely chopped
1 green pepper, chopped
1/4 t. garlic powder

1/2 t. salt
2 c. chicken broth
1 c. long-cooking rice, uncooked
1-1/2 c. cooked chicken, cubed
Optional: 1 T. chopped green
    olives, drained

Melt butter in a large skillet over medium heat. Add tomatoes, onion, green pepper and seasonings; simmer for about 5 minutes. Stir in chicken broth and uncooked rice. Cover and simmer over low heat for 18 to 20 minutes, until broth is absorbed and rice is tender. Add chicken and olives, if using; heat through and serve. Makes 5 servings.

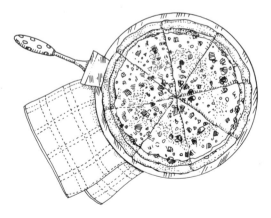

Turn leftovers into pizza! Top a ready-to-bake crust with pizza sauce, sliced baked chicken or grilled steak, veggies and whatever sounds good to you. Finish with a sprinkle of cheese and bake until hot and bubbly, about 10 minutes at 400 degrees. Yummy!

Suppers
in a Snap

Texas Chicken & Chiles

Caroline Mahoney
Valencia, PA

*We just love this recipe...it has great flavor! It's even better
the next day. To reduce fat, use low-fat cheese and
sour cream...it'll still be delicious.*

4 boneless, skinless chicken
    breasts, cut in half
1-1/4 oz. pkg. taco seasoning
    mix
1/4 c. sliced black olives, drained
2 T. canned green chiles, drained

2 green onions, sliced
14-1/2 oz. can Mexican-style
    stewed tomatoes
1/2 c. shredded Cheddar cheese
Garnish: sour cream

Arrange chicken breasts in a lightly greased roasting pan. Sprinkle
chicken with seasoning mix; top with olives, chiles and onions. Spoon
tomatoes with juice around chicken; sprinkle with cheese. Cover with
aluminum foil. Bake at 350 degrees for 45 to 60 minutes, until heated
through and chicken juices run clear. Serve chicken topped with dollops
of sour cream. Makes 4 servings.

Fix a double batch! Brown 2 pounds of ground beef with
2 packages of taco seasoning mix, then freeze half of the mixture
for a quick meal of tacos or taco salad another night.

Italian Skillet Chicken

JoAnn
Gooseberry Patch

Flavorful and so simple. Serve the chicken and pan sauce
over cooked rice or thin spaghetti...yum!

8 chicken thighs
1/2 t. salt
1/2 t. pepper
1 T. olive oil
2 c. onions, chopped

4 cloves garlic, minced
1-1/2 t. dried thyme
2 14-1/2 oz. cans diced tomatoes
    with basil, garlic & oregano

Remove skin from chicken thighs, if desired; season with salt and pepper. Heat oil in a Dutch oven over medium-high heat. Add chicken to skillet, a few pieces at a time; cook for 5 minutes per side. Remove chicken from pan; set aside. Add onions, garlic and thyme to drippings in pan. Cook over medium heat until onions are soft, stirring often. Add tomato juice from one can. Continue to cook and stir, scraping up browned bits from bottom of pan, until juice evaporates. Add tomatoes from both cans with remaining juice; return chicken to pan. Bring to a simmer; reduce heat to medium-low. Cover and simmer for 20 minutes or until chicken juices run clear. Serve chicken topped with sauce from pan. Makes 8 servings.

Polenta is a terrific side dish for saucy Italian dishes. Topped with marinara sauce and sautéed mushrooms, it can even serve as a meatless main dish. Look for tubes of ready-to-use polenta in the supermarket's refrigerated section...easy to slice, heat and serve.

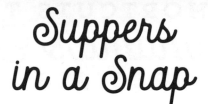

Suppers in a Snap

Fried Cabbage & Noodles with Smoked Sausage

Linda Knox
Niota, TN

Try your favorite sausage in this easy skillet meal.

12-oz. pkg. extra-wide egg
  noodles, uncooked
1 lb. smoked pork sausage, cut
  into chunks

1/2 c. butter
1 head cabbage, quartered
  and sliced
salt and pepper to taste

Cook pasta according to package directions, adding sausage 2 to
3 minutes before pasta is done. Drain pasta mixture and set aside.
Meanwhile, melt butter in a large skillet over low heat. Increase heat to
medium; add cabbage. Cover and cook, stirring often, until cabbage
cooks down. Season with salt and pepper. Stir pasta mixture into
cabbage and serve. Makes 4 servings.

Mother's Stuffed Peppers

Ida Mannion
North Chelmsford, MA

*My mother would make these for us and we all loved them.
If your kids don't care for green peppers, try milder
red or yellow peppers.*

4 to 5 green peppers, halved
1 to 1-1/2 lbs. ground beef
6.8-oz. pkg. Spanish rice
  vermicelli mix, uncooked

14-1/2 oz. can stewed tomatoes

Add peppers to a saucepan of boiling water; cook for 5 minutes. Drain
peppers cut-side down on paper towels. Meanwhile, brown beef in a
skillet over medium heat; drain. In another saucepan, prepare Spanish
rice according to package directions. Add beef and tomatoes with
juice to cooked rice; mix well. Arrange peppers in a lightly greased
13"x9" baking pan. Spoon mixture into peppers, filling loosely. Bake,
uncovered, at 350 degrees for 35 to 45 minutes. Serves 4 to 5.

Burgundy Beef

Debi King
Reisterstown, MD

My mom belonged to a monthly luncheon club. One day over forty years ago, she came home from the club with this recipe. I've modified it for the slow cooker and added some carrots. It's delicious served with a crisp salad, bread and Mississippi mud pie for dessert.

2 lbs. stew beef cubes
1 lb. sliced mushrooms
1/2 c. baby carrots
2 10-3/4 oz. cans golden
   mushroom soup

3/4 c. Burgundy wine or
   beef broth
2 T. onion soup mix
cooked egg noodles or rice

In a 4-quart slow cooker, combine all ingredients except noodles or rice; stir gently. Cover and cook on high setting for 3 to 4 hours, or on low setting for 6 to 8 hours, until beef is very tender. Stir again. To serve, ladle beef mixture over cooked noodles or rice. Makes 4 servings.

Making baked potatoes for the whole family? Stand 'em up
in a muffin pan...easy in and out of the oven. Bake at
400 degrees for 50 minutes to one hour, until fork-tender.

Suppers in a Snap

Slow-Cooker Ravioli Lasagna

*Joyce Roebuck
Jacksonville, TX*

*That's right, no noodles! This recipe uses frozen ravioli instead.
It's so easy and everyone loves it...try it and you'll see! Toss a
salad, make some garlic bread and there's your meal.*

1 lb. ground beef
24-oz. jar marinara or
  spaghetti sauce
8-oz. can tomato sauce
Italian seasoning to taste

13-oz. pkg. frozen 3-cheese
  ravioli, uncooked
1 c. shredded mozzarella cheese
1 c. shredded Parmesan cheese

Brown beef in a skillet over medium heat; drain. Stir in sauces and
seasoning. In a 4-quart slow cooker, layer half of beef mixture, half of
uncooked ravioli and half of each cheese. Repeat layering, ending with
cheeses. Cover and cook on low setting for 4 hours, or until bubbly and
heated through. Makes 4 servings.

To grate or shred a block of cheese easily,
freeze the wrapped cheese for 10 to 20 minutes...
it will just glide across the grater!

Quick Hawaiian Pizza

Paula Marchesi
Auburn, PA

When you're running late and need to make something for dinner, this is quick, simple and very tasty. I like to keep these ingredients on hand for busy nights when I say to myself, "Oh no, what's for dinner?" It's a good use for leftover cooked chicken, if you have some.

8-oz. tube refrigerated
    crescent rolls
1/2 c. honey barbecue sauce
6-oz. pkg. grilled chicken
    breast strips

1 c. canned pineapple tidbits,
    drained
1-1/2 c. shredded Mexican-blend
    cheese

Unroll crescent rolls into a greased 13"x9" inch baking pan; seal seams and perforations. Bake at 375 degrees for 6 to 8 minutes, until golden. Spread sauce over baked crust; top with chicken, pineapple and cheese. Bake, uncovered, for 12 to 15 minutes, until heated through and cheese is melted. Makes 6 servings.

Party time! Kids love make-your-own bars...set up the makings for pizza, tacos or ice cream sundaes and let 'em do it themselves!

Suppers in a Snap

Baked Marinated Hot Dogs

Tammy Navarro
Littleton, CO

This is a different take on hot dogs. It's an easy after-school snack or dinner. My kids and grandkids enjoy them...I like them, too!

8 hot dogs
1/4 c. catsup
2 T. Worcestershire sauce

1 T. garlic, minced, or to taste
8 hot dog buns, split

Cut 3 slits in each hot dog on both sides; don't cut all the way through. Add hot dogs to a large plastic zipping bag; set aside. Combine catsup, Worcestershire sauce and garlic in a cup; mix well and add to bag. Seal bag; roll hot dogs in sauce until well coated. Refrigerate hot dogs in bag at least 30 minutes, or up to 2 hours. Line a rimmed baking sheet with aluminum foil; spray lightly with non-stick vegetable spray. Arrange hot dogs on pan. Bake at 350 degrees for 15 to 20 minutes, turning once. Serve hot dogs in buns. Makes 8 servings.

French Fried Casserole

Bev Traxler
British Columbia, Canada

My grandkids and many adults love this casserole. It's delicious, and a snap to make! Serve with a platter of fresh vegetables.

1 lb. lean ground beef
10-3/4 oz. can Cheddar
cheese soup

10-3/4 oz. can golden
mushroom soup
20-oz. pkg. frozen French fries

Press uncooked beef into a lightly greased 13"x9" baking pan; set aside. Stir together soups in a bowl; spread over beef. Top generously with frozen French fries. Bake, uncovered, at 350 degrees for one hour and 15 minutes, until beef is browned and French fries are crisp and golden. Makes 4 servings.

Faux Fried Rice with Chicken
Constance Bockstoce
Dallas, GA

I changed out rice for cauliflower rice in this recipe...it suited my low-carb needs as well as my daughter's diabetic needs and my son's palate for some tasty fried rice. It was a hit for us all!

2 T. olive oil
14-oz. pkg. shredded
   coleslaw mix
12-oz. pkg. frozen
   cauliflower rice
2 boneless, skinless chicken
   breasts, cooked and diced

1/2 c. frozen peas
3 T. soy sauce
1-1/2 t. ground ginger
1/2 t. garlic powder
1/2 t. onion powder
1/2 t. pepper
1 egg, beaten

Heat olive oil in a non-stick skillet over medium-high heat. Add coleslaw mix and cauliflower rice; sauté for 3 to 5 minutes, stirring often. Add chicken, frozen peas, soy sauce and seasonings. Cook for another 3 minutes, or until heated through. Make 4 wells in mixture with a spoon; divide beaten egg among wells. Reduce heat to medium-low. Cover and cook for 2 minutes; stir. Continue cooking just until egg is set and serve. Serves 2 to 4.

A super-simple, whimsical dessert to serve after an Asian meal!
Scoop rainbow sherbet into stemmed glasses, then slip
a fortune cookie over the edge of each glass.

Suppers in a Snap

Beef & Vegetable Stir-Fry

Kay Marone
Des Moines, IA

*A favorite one-dish dinner! We like to top it with
crispy chow mein noodles.*

2 t. cornstarch
1 c. water
2 T. soy sauce
1 T. roasted garlic &
    pepper seasoning
1/2 t. ground ginger

1 T. oil
1-1/2 lbs. boneless beef sirloin,
    cut into thin strips
3 c. frozen sugar snap pea
    stir-fry blend
cooked rice

In a cup, stir together cornstarch, water, soy sauce and seasonings until smooth; set aside. Heat oil in a large skillet over medium-high heat. Working in batches, add beef strips; cook and stir for 5 minutes, or until no longer pink. Add frozen vegetables to skillet; cook and stir for 4 to 5 minutes, until tender. Return beef to skillet. Add cornstarch to skillet. Bring to a boil, stirring constantly; boil for one minute, or until thickened. Serve mixture ladled over cooked rice. Serves 6.

Cut beef, chicken or pork into thin strips or slices
in a snap! Just pop the meat into the freezer
for 20 to 30 minutes before slicing.

Smothered Pork Chops

Jason Keller
Carrollton, GA

Grandma used to make the most delicious smothered pork chops using the juicy tomatoes she grew in her garden. Seasoned, canned tomatoes speed things up a little, but the taste is still pure comfort.

14-1/2 oz. can diced tomatoes
  with garlic & onion
1 t. Worcestershire sauce
1/2 t. sugar
2 T. olive oil, divided

1 c. onion, diced
4 bone-in pork chops, cut
  one-inch thick
salt and coarse pepper to taste

In a bowl, combine tomatoes with juice, Worcestershire sauce and sugar; stir well and set aside. Heat one tablespoon oil in a large skillet over medium-high heat; add onion. Cook until deeply golden, stirring occasionally, about 8 minutes. Add onion to tomato mixture; set aside. Heat remaining oil in skillet. Season pork chops on both sides with salt and pepper; add to skillet and cook for 2 minutes. Turn chops over; spoon tomato mixture over chops and bring to a boil. Reduce heat to medium. Cover and simmer for 20 minutes, or until tender. Remove chops to a serving platter, reserving sauce in skillet. Simmer sauce over medium-high heat for about 5 minutes, until slightly thickened. Spoon sauce over chops and serve. Serves 4.

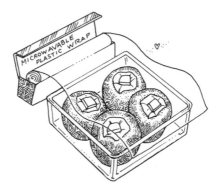

Microwaved baked apples are an easy side dish. Core apples nearly through; add a teaspoon each of butter and brown sugar. Place in a microwave-safe dish, cover with plastic wrap and microwave on high setting for 3 to 6 minutes, until tender.

Gravified Chicken

Dawn Raskiewicz
Alliance, NE

I love anything with gravy on it, but my husband really doesn't care for gravy. This is one dish he loves and will eat...as long as I never use the word gravy! Serve with mashed potatoes, covering them with the gravy from the skillet. For a vegetable choice, we enjoy sweet corn on the cob and a zesty tossed salad.

4 to 6 chicken thighs
1 c. all-purpose flour
seasoned salt and pepper
    to taste
oil for frying
2-oz. pkg. chicken noodle
    soup mix

10-3/4 oz. can cream of
    chicken soup
1-1/4 c. milk
1 t. garlic powder

Dredge chicken thighs in flour; sprinkle with seasoned salt and pepper as desired. Heat oil in a large skillet over medium heat. Add chicken to skillet and simmer until tender and nearly done, turning occasionally. Sprinkle noodle soup mix over chicken. In a bowl, whisk together chicken soup, milk and garlic powder; spoon over chicken. Simmer for 15 to 20 minutes, turning chicken once and occasionally stirring gravy. Makes 4 to 6 servings.

Mix flour and seasonings for dredging meat on a piece of
wax paper...when you're done, just toss it away.

Mom's Steak Spaghetti

Sue Hartsough
Urichsville, OH

My mother used to make this yummy dish when I was growing up. We kids asked her to make it for our birthdays. It was always a big hit!

1 lb. spaghetti, uncooked
1-1/2 lbs. ground beef
3/4 c. onion, chopped
1 green pepper, chopped
3 10-3/4 oz. cans tomato soup
2-1/2 c. water

1/2 t. salt
1/4 t. pepper
3 c. pasteurized process cheese,
　cubed
Garnish: grated Parmesan cheese

Cook spaghetti according to package directions; drain and return to pan. Meanwhile, in a skillet over medium heat, brown beef with onion and green pepper; drain. Add beef mixture to cooked spaghetti. Add tomato soup, water, salt and pepper; mix well. Fold in cheese. Transfer mixture to a lightly greased 4-quart casserole dish. Bake, covered, at 350 degrees for one hour. Sprinkle with Parmesan cheese and serve. Serves 6 to 8.

Be a savvy shopper. Make a shopping list, grouping items by the area of the store where they're found...produce, meats, canned goods and frozen foods. You'll breeze right down the aisles.

Suppers in a Snap

Polish Kielbasa & Pierogies

Samantha Starks
Madison, WI

*Just four ingredients for this hearty skillet meal. We enjoy it
with steamed and buttered zucchini or yellow squash.*

2 16-oz. pkgs. frozen potato
   pierogies, uncooked
14-oz. pkg. Kielbasa sausage

2 T. butter
1 onion, thinly sliced

In a Dutch oven, cook pierogies according to package directions. Drain;
cover to keep warm. Meanwhile, brown sausage in a large skillet over
medium heat. Remove sausage from skillet; allow to cool slightly and
slice. Melt butter in skillet over medium heat, cook onion until tender.
Return sausage to skillet; cook and stir until sausage is heated through.
Stir in pierogies and serve. Makes 6 servings.

Mashed potatoes can't be beat! Save time peeling and cooking...
warm up refrigerated mashed potatoes and top with shredded
cheese, bacon bits and green onions, for loaded potatoes
in a hurry. Scrumptious!

Deviled Tuna Casserole

Kim McCallie
Guyton, GA

The first time my husband tasted this casserole, he thought he was eating crabmeat instead of tuna! It's perfect for those who are on a budget and are cooking from the pantry.

16-oz. pkg. elbow macaroni, uncooked
6-oz. can white tuna in water, drained and flaked
2 10-3/4 oz. cans cream of chicken soup
14-1/2 oz. can chicken broth
2 T. Dijon mustard
4 to 5 drops hot pepper sauce
1 t. seafood seasoning
1/4 t. paprika
1/4 t. seasoning salt
1/4 t. garlic salt
1/4 t. pepper
1/4 c. dry bread crumbs
2 T. butter, sliced
Garnish additional paprika

Cook macaroni according to package directions; drain. Meanwhile, combine remaining ingredients except bread crumbs, butter and garnish in a large bowl; mix well. Fold in cooked macaroni. Spread mixture in a greased 3-quart casserole dish. Sprinkle with bread crumbs; dot with butter and sprinkle with additional paprika. Bake, uncovered, at 350 degrees for 30 minutes, or until hot and bubbly. Makes 6 servings.

Write your most-used recipes on 4"x6" index cards...they'll fit perfectly into a mini photo album. The plastic pages will protect your recipes from spatters and you'll save time finding the recipe you need.

Suppers in a Snap

Alfredo Salmon & Noodles

Carolyn Deckard
Bedford, IN

*My husband loves salmon any way I fix it. I got this easy recipe
from a sweet lady at work. He liked it so well that now
we have it for dinner once a month.*

3 c. wide egg noodles, uncooked
10-oz. pkg. frozen chopped
  broccoli
1/2 c. jarred Alfredo sauce

6-oz. can boneless, skinless pink
  salmon, drained and flaked
1/8 t. pepper

Cook noodles according to package directions, adding broccoli to pan for
the last 4 to 5 minutes of cooktime. Drain; return noodle mixture to pan.
Stir in remaining ingredients. Cook over low heat for 4 to 6 minutes,
stirring occasionally, until heated through. Makes 4 servings.

There is only one difference between a long life
and a good dinner...that, in the dinner,
the sweets come last.
–Robert Louis Stevenson

Wendy's Taco Rice

Wendy Ball
Battle Creek, MI

I've served this dish as an after-holiday meal. Sometimes, because our family is so large and scheduling gatherings is difficult, we have to spread out our family events. So this is a nice change from a traditional meal and it's quick to make. It may just be our new after-holiday meal! The important thing is just getting together to spend time with each other.

1 lb. ground beef
3/4 c. onion, chopped
16-oz. jar favorite salsa
1 c. beef or chicken broth
1 c. water
1-1/4 oz. pkg. taco seasoning
   mix
15-1/2 oz. can black beans,
   drained and rinsed

1-1/2 c. instant brown rice,
   uncooked
tortilla chips
Garnish: salsa, shredded cheese,
   sour cream, sliced black
   olives, green onions

In a skillet over medium heat, cook beef with onion until beef is no longer pink; drain. Stir in salsa, broth, water and seasoning mix; bring to a boil. Reduce heat to medium-low; cover and simmer for 5 minutes. Stir in beans and uncooked rice. Cover and simmer for 25 to 30 minutes until rice is tender, stirring occasionally. Serve with tortilla chips; garnish as desired. Makes 4 to 6 servings.

Wide-rimmed soup plates are perfect for serving up saucy pasta and rice dishes, as well as hearty dinner portions of soup. Balance a hot roll or a slice of bread on the rim...no bread plate needed!

Suppers in a Snap

Light-Speed Tamale Casserole

Cindy Kemp
Benton, AR

I came up with this recipe several years ago, when my daughters were little. The weather was bad that day, so I searched out what was available in the pantry. This ridiculously delicious dinner was the result! Serve with a crisp salad and buttered corn. This is absolutely wonderful the next day, too!

2 c. corn or tortilla chips, crushed and divided
15-1/2 oz. can chili beans or pork & beans
28-oz. can favorite tamales in chili sauce

15-oz. can favorite chili, or 2 c. homemade chili
8-oz. pkg. shredded Cheddar cheese

Spray a 3-quart oblong casserole dish with non-stick vegetable spray. Spread one cup crushed chips in dish; spoon beans with liquid over chips and set aside. Open tamale can and unwrap tamales. Arrange whole or sliced tamales over beans. Spoon chili sauce from can over tamales; spread chili over tamales. Top with cheese and remaining chips; cover with aluminum foil. Bake at 350 degrees for 45 minutes, or until lightly golden and cheese is melted and gooey. Remove foil during last 5 minutes. Let stand for for 15 to 20 minutes before serving. Makes 6 to 8 servings.

A speedy side for a south-of-the-border supper. Stir spicy salsa and shredded cheese into hot cooked rice. Cover and let stand a few minutes, until the cheese melts. Sure to please!

Light Chicken Italiano

Pattie Woods
Coshocton, OH

Something different...it's delicious and takes just a moment to fix. Try different flavors of bread crumbs and salad dressing for a change.

1/2 c. Italian salad dressing
1-1/2 c. Italian-seasoned
   dry bread crumbs
4 chicken breasts

1/2 onion, sliced
1 ripe tomato, sliced
2 cloves garlic, minced

Pour salad dressing into a shallow bowl; add bread crumbs to another shallow bowl. Dip chicken breasts into salad dressing, then into bread crumbs, coating well. Arrange chicken in a lightly greased 13"x9" baking pan; top with onion, tomato and garlic. Drizzle any remaining salad dressing over chicken. Bake, uncovered, at 375 degrees for 35 to 40 minutes, until chicken juices run clear when pierced. Makes 4 servings.

Flattened boneless chicken breasts cook up quickly and evenly. Simply place chicken between 2 pieces of plastic wrap and gently pound to desired thickness with a meat mallet or a small skillet.

Suppers in a Snap

Italian Salsa Chicken

Amanda Porter
North Ogden, UT

When I visited my sister, I made this dish for her family. My brother-in-law loved it...he was just sad that there was only enough left over for one day's lunch! Served with cooked rice or pasta, and a fresh vegetable, it's a nice meal.

4 to 6 boneless, skinless chicken
   breasts
16-oz. jar favorite salsa

8-oz. bottle Italian salad dressing
cooked rice or pasta

Arrange chicken breasts in a lightly greased 5-quart slow cooker; top with salsa and salad dressing. Cover and cook on low setting for 4 to 6 hours. If desired, shred chicken and stir back into mixture in slow cooker. Serve with cooked rice or pasta. Serves 4 to 6.

Baked Buttermilk Chicken

Sandy Ward
Anderson, IN

I love fixing chicken thighs as a main dish. They are juicy and flavorful! Serve with buttered pasta of your choice and a simple salad, with warm Italian bread to top it off.

1/2 c. buttermilk
1 c. Italian-seasoned dry
   bread crumbs

8 boneless, skinless chicken
   thighs

Add buttermilk to a shallow bowl; add bread crumbs to another shallow bowl. Dip chicken thighs into buttermilk; roll in bread crumbs. Arrange in a lightly greased 13"x9" baking pan. Bake, uncovered, at 350 degrees for one hour, or until tender. Serves 4.

Prevent messy pasta boil-overs! Rub a little vegetable oil over
the top few inches inside the cooking pot.

Pork Chop & Hashbrown Casserole

Shirley Howie
Foxboro, MA

The prep time for this tasty dish is short...it makes great leftovers for the next day, too!

5 to 6 pork chops
1 T. oil
1 c. sour cream
10-3/4 oz. can cream of
   celery soup

1/2 c. milk
32-oz. pkg. frozen diced
   hashbrowns, thawed
1 c. onion, chopped
1 c. shredded Cheddar cheese

In a large skillet over medium heat, brown pork chops in oil on both sides. Drain; set aside. In a large bowl, combine sour cream, celery soup and milk; stir in hashbrowns and onion. Spread sour cream mixture in a lightly greased 13" x 9" baking pan. Sprinkle with cheese; arrange pork chops on top. Cover with aluminum foil. Bake at 350 degrees for 45 to 50 minutes. Remove foil and bake for 10 minutes longer, or until heated through and chops are fully cooked. Makes 5 to 6 servings.

Keep some festive paper plates and napkins tucked away...
they'll set a lighthearted mood on busy evenings,
with easy clean-up afterwards.

Suppers in a Snap

Chicken Noodle Casserole

Hazel Palmer
West Milton, OH

*Whenever we have special dinners, I like to make this casserole.
Afterwards, the dish is always empty! Try it with
chicken & rice soup mix too.*

4.2-oz. pkg. chicken noodle
  soup mix
2 10-3/4 oz. cans cream of
  mushroom soup
1 c. sour cream

1/4 c. grated Parmesan cheese
salt and pepper to taste
2 to 3 c. cooked chicken, chopped
1 to 2 c. favorite shredded cheese

In a large saucepan, prepare soup mix as package directs. Whisk in
mushroom soup, sour cream, Parmesan cheese, salt and pepper. Fold in
chicken; spoon mixture into a 13"x9" baking pan. Bake, uncovered, at
350 degrees for 30 minutes, or until hot and bubbly. Top with shredded
cheese; return to oven until cheese melts. Makes 8 servings.

No cream of mushroom soup in the pantry? Cream of celery
or chicken is sure to be just as tasty...you may even discover
a new way you like even better!

Southern Chicken Pot Pie

Kathy Garland
Cannon, KY

I serve this tasty pot pie with tossed salad and applesauce
or pudding for a quick meal.

2 12-1/2 oz. cans chunk white
   chicken, drained and flaked
2 29-oz. cans mixed vegetables,
   drained
10-3/4 oz. can cream of
   chicken soup

10-3/4 oz. can cream of
   celery soup
1-1/4 c. milk
2 8-1/2 oz. pkgs. corn
   muffin mix

Combine all ingredients except corn muffin mix in a lightly greased
13"x9" baking pan; mix well and set aside. Prepare corn muffin mix
according to package instructions; spoon batter over mixture in pan.
Bake, uncovered, at 350 degrees for 25 to 35 minutes, until cornbread
is set and golden. Makes 8 servings.

Country Chicken & Dumplings

Caroline Britt
Cleveland, TX

When you're facing hard times, nothing is better than
creamy chicken & dumplings.

8 chicken thighs
4 c. baby carrots, halved
1 onion, chopped
2 to 3 7-1/2 oz. tubes
   refrigerated biscuits,
   quartered

1/3 c. evaporated milk
salt and pepper to taste

In a stockpot, cover chicken, carrots and onion with water. Bring to a
boil over high heat. Reduce heat to medium-low; cover and simmer for
10 to 12 minutes, until chicken is no longer pink in the center. Remove
chicken; cut into cubes and set aside, discarding skin and bones. Drop
biscuits into boiling broth in stockpot. Simmer over low heat until
dumplings are cooked through and fluffy inside. Return chicken to
pan along with milk, salt and pepper; heat through. Serves 8 to 10.

Speedy Cookies & Desserts

Chocolate Dream Dessert

Charlotte Smith
Huntingdon, PA

This recipe is so easy and very good! A nice dessert to take to a picnic or church dinner. If you don't have two 13"x9" pans, you can layer it all in a pretty glass serving bowl.

18-1/2 oz. pkg. chocolate
   cake mix
3.4-oz. pkg. instant vanilla
   pudding mix
2 c. milk

1 c. chocolate syrup, divided
12-oz. container frozen whipped
   topping, thawed
1/2 c. chopped pecans

Prepare cake mix according to package directions; bake in a greased 13"x9" baking pan. Cool in pan on a wire rack. Meanwhile, in a large bowl, whisk together pudding mix and milk for 2 minutes. Spoon evenly into a separate ungreased 13"x9" baking pan. Tear cake into small pieces and gently push down into pudding. Drizzle with 3/4 cup chocolate syrup; spread with whipped topping. Drizzle with remaining syrup; sprinkle with pecans. Cover and refrigerate until serving time. Makes 12 to 15 servings.

Need a yummy dessert for a crowd? Sheet cakes and trifle bowls go together in a jiffy...easy to serve, too! Dress 'em up for a special occasion with colorful candy sprinkles.

Speedy Cookies & Desserts

Blueberry Nut Crunch

Joyce Borrill
Utica, NY

Easy, simple and delicious...why not make one today?

18-1/4 oz. pkg. yellow cake mix
1 pt. blueberries
20-oz. can crushed pineapple,
    drained
3/4 c. butter, melted
1/2 c. chopped nuts

Prepare cake mix according to package directions. Mix blueberries and pineapple into batter; spread in a greased 13"x9" baking pan. Drizzle with melted butter; sprinkle with nuts. Bake at 350 degrees for one hour. Cut into squares to serve. Makes 10 servings.

Toasted oats can take the place of chopped nuts in cakes and cookies, adding crunch and nutty flavor. Simply cook uncooked oats in a little butter until golden. Cool before adding to a recipe.

Mandarin Orange Pie

Janis Parr
Ontario, Canada

This scrumptious pie is a refreshing change from apple pie and the usual berry varieties. Goes together in minutes, too!

2 8-oz. pkgs. cream cheese, softened
14-oz. can sweetened condensed milk
11-oz. can mandarin oranges, drained

1/4 c. chopped pecans
8-oz. container frozen whipped topping, thawed
9-inch graham cracker or shortbread crust

In a large bowl, blend together cream cheese and condensed milk. Add oranges and pecans; stir gently to combine. Fold in whipped topping. Spoon mixture into crust. Cover and chill well; cut into wedges. Makes 6 to 8 servings.

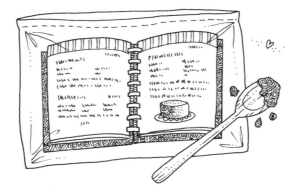

Keep your favorite cookbook spatter-free and open to the page you're using! Just slide it inside a gallon-size plastic zipping bag.

Speedy Cookies & Desserts

Apricot-Almond Bars

Sandra Mirando
Depew, NY

This is one of the best non-chocolate bars I have ever tried and it is so easy to make, starting with a cake mix. Be sure to use the golden butter-flavored cake mix.

1 c. all-purpose flour
15-1/2 oz. golden butter
 cake mix
3/4 c. butter, softened

1 c. sliced almonds
1 c. flaked coconut
12-oz. jar apricot preserves

In a large bowl, combine flour and dry cake mix; mix well and cut in butter. Add almonds and coconut; mix well. Pat 2/3 of mixture into an ungreased 13"x9" baking pan. Spread apricot preserves over mixture. Crumble remaining flour mixture over preserves. Bake at 325 degrees for one hour, or until lightly golden. Cool; cut into bars. Makes 2 dozen.

Quick Pudding Cookies

Linda Crandall
Pulaski, NY

Back in 1970, a fellow service wife shared this recipe with me, and my two daughters enjoyed the cookies. It's still a fun recipe.

3.4-oz. favorite-flavor cook &
 serve pudding mix
1 c. biscuit baking mix

1/4 c. oil
3 T. water
1 egg, lightly beaten

In a bowl, combine dry pudding and biscuit mixes; stir well. Add oil, water and egg; mix well. Drop dough by teaspoonfuls onto ungreased baking sheets. Bake at 375 degrees for 12 minutes. Cool cookies on wire racks. Makes about 2-1/2 dozen.

Save time when baking...tuck measuring cups into your
countertop canisters, ready to scoop out flour and sugar
when you need them.

Slow-Cooker Preacher's Delight
Nancy Lanning
Lancaster, SC

My husband is a pastor, and when our kids were young, they loved making this dessert. It's easy and yummy, and was always ready for us in the slow cooker when we got back from church for dinner. Use any fruit pie filling you like...apple, peach or blueberry, or mix them up!

2 21-oz. cans cherry pie filling
18-1/2 oz. pkg. yellow cake mix
1/2 c. butter, melted

Optional: 1/2 c. chopped walnuts
Garnish: vanilla ice cream or
   whipped cream

Spray a 3 to 4-quart slow cooker with non-stick vegetable spray. Add pie filling to slow cooker; set aside. Stir together dry cake mix and butter in a bowl; mixture will be crumbly. Sprinkle over filling. Sprinkle with walnuts, if desired. Cover and cook on low setting for 2 to 3 hours. To serve, spoon into bowls; top with ice cream or whipped cream. Makes 8 servings.

Come and share my pot of tea,
my home is warm and my friendship's free.

–Emilie Barnes

Speedy Cookies & Desserts

Lynnette's Strawberry Cake

Lynnette Jones
East Flat Rock, NC

This is a super-easy cake with lots of shortcuts!
It's scrumptious, too.

1/2 c. boiling water
6-oz. pkg. strawberry gelatin mix
2 10-oz. pkgs. frozen
   strawberries in syrup, thawed

3 8-oz. containers frozen
   whipped topping, thawed
   and divided
1 angel food cake

In a large bowl, combine boiling water and gelatin mix; stir for 2 minutes, or until dissolved. Add strawberries with syrup to gelatin; mix well. Cover and refrigerate until thickened. Fold 2-1/2 containers whipped topping into strawberry mixture; set aside. (Remaining topping may be used for another recipe.) Slice cake horizontally into 3 layers; place bottom layer on a cake plate. Assemble cake, spreading strawberry mixture between cake layers. Frost the outside of cake with remaining strawberry mixture. Cover and refrigerate until serving time; slice to serve. Serves 10 to 12.

Turn your favorite cake recipe into cupcakes...easy to serve, fun to eat! Fill greased muffin cups 2/3 full. Bake at the same temperature as in the recipe, but cut the baking time by 1/3 to 1/2. You'll get 24 to 30 cupcakes from a 2-layer cake recipe.

Crescent Pecan Pie Bars

Karen Wilson
Defiance, OH

These delicious bars use a shortcut of refrigerated crescent rolls for the crust. Why not treat your family today?

8-oz. tube refrigerated
   crescent rolls
1 egg, beaten
1/2 c. sugar
1/2 c. corn syrup

1 T. butter, melted
1 t. vanilla extract
1/2 t. salt
1 c. chopped pecans

Unroll crescent rolls and lay flat in a lightly greased 13"x9" baking pan. Press to cover bottom of the pan; press up to form a 3/4-inch rim. Bake at 375 degrees for 5 minutes. In a bowl, stir together egg, sugar, corn syrup, melted butter, vanilla and salt. Fold in pecans; spoon mixture over baked crust. Bake at 375 degrees for 18 to 22 minutes, until golden. Cool; cut into squares. Makes 2 dozen.

Grandma always said, "Never return a dish empty." Gather up casseroles and pie plates that have been left behind, fill them with homemade cookies and return to their owners!

Speedy Cookies & Desserts

Cinnamon-Pecan Cookies

Ellen Folkman
Crystal Beach, FL

These cookies are great for cookie exchanges and bake sales.
A dear friend shared the recipe with me years ago.

18-oz. pkg. refrigerated sugar
   cookie dough
2 t. cinnamon

2 t. vanilla extract
1-1/2 c. chopped pecans

Break up cookie dough into a large bowl; let stand for 10 to 15 minutes to soften. Add cinnamon, vanilla and chopped pecans; beat with an electric mixer with paddle attachment on medium speed. Drop dough by teaspoonfuls onto parchment paper-lined baking sheets, 2 inches apart. Bake at 350 degrees for 10 to 12 minutes, just until set and golden at edges. Remove from oven; cool on baking sheets for 2 minutes. Transfer to a wire rack; cool completely. Makes 2 dozen.

Julie's Apricot Cake

Julie Perkins
Anderson, IN

I love making this cake for showers, Easter and Sunday dinners.

18-1/4 oz. pkg. lemon cake mix
15-oz. can apricot halves in
   juice, chopped

3 eggs, lightly beaten
Optional: 1 c. apricot jam

In a large bowl, combine dry cake mix, apricots with juice and eggs; mix well. Pour batter into a greased and floured 13"x9" baking pan. Bake at 350 degrees for 30 to 35 minutes, until a toothpick inserted in the center tests done. If desired, spread cake with apricot jam while still warm. Cut into squares. Makes 12 to 15 servings.

Life is uncertain...eat dessert first!
–Ernestine Ulmer

Spiced Peach Cobbler

Nancy Kailihiwa
Wheatland, CA

I couldn't believe how simple this recipe was, and yet how absolutely delicious it was. I keep the ingredients on hand so I can always whip up a quick dessert for unexpected guests or a last-minute addition to a church gathering.

2 29-oz. cans sliced peaches
    in 100% juice, divided
1 T. cinnamon
18-1/4 oz. pkg. spice cake mix

3/4 c. butter, sliced
Garnish: whipped topping or
    vanilla ice cream

Coat a 13"x9" baking pan with non-stick vegetable spray; add one can peaches with juice to pan. Drain the remaining can and add peaches to pan. Sprinkle cinnamon over peaches; mix to combine. Sprinkle dry cake mix over peaches; spread cake mix over peaches and to the edges of pan. Do not stir. Top evenly with sliced butter. Bake at 375 degrees for 35 minutes, or until cake is set and golden. Let cool to room temperature. Serve with whipped topping or ice cream. Makes 10 servings.

Serving ice cream is a snap...place scoops in a paper-lined muffin tin and freeze. At dessert time, each scoop will be all ready to top pie à la mode or place beside slices of cake.

Speedy Cookies & Desserts

Frosted Apple Cake

Angela Sargent
Princeton, WV

I came up with this quick & easy dessert on a crisp fall afternoon when my family needed something sweet. Top it with a handful of candy sprinkles for a colorful touch.

18-1/4 oz. pkg. yellow cake mix
2 Honeycrisp apples, peeled,
   cored and diced
1/2 c. brown sugar, packed
1 t. cinnamon

16-oz. container buttercream
   frosting
1/2 t. sugar
1/2 t. apple pie spice

Prepare cake mix according to package directions. Add apples, brown sugar and cinnamon; mix gently until well blended. Pour batter into a greased 13"x9" baking pan. Bake at 350 degrees for 25 minutes, or until a toothpick inserted in the center tests clean. Cool completely; spread with frosting. Combine sugar and spice in a cup; sprinkle over frosted cake. Cut into squares. Makes 8 to 10 servings.

Upgrade any boxed cake mix quickly! Simply add
an extra egg and use melted butter in place of the oil
called for in the directions.

Quick Coconut Cream Pie

Lisa Tucker
Dunbar, WV

My grandmother's favorite pie was coconut cream. This recipe is the easiest one I have found...our family enjoys its terrific flavor!

5.1-oz. pkg. instant vanilla
   pudding mix
1-1/2 c. cold milk
1 c. flaked coconut, toasted
   and divided

8-oz. container frozen whipped
   topping, thawed and divided
9-inch graham cracker crust

In a large bowl, combine pudding mix and milk; beat with an electric mixer on medium-low speed for 2 minutes. Fold in 3/4 cup coconut and half of whipped topping; spoon into crust. Sprinkle with remaining coconut. Cover and chill until set. Cut into wedges; garnish with remaining topping. Makes 6 to 8 servings.

To toast coconut: Spread flaked coconut evenly on a parchment
paper-lined baking sheet. Bake at 325 degrees for 3 minutes;
stir gently with a spatula. Bake another 3 to 4 minutes,
until coconut is golden.

Speedy Cookies & Desserts

Grandma's Banana Pudding

Amanda Tlachac
Chicago, IL

*My grandmother always made this for us at Christmastime.
It's so easy and so good...give it a try!*

3 c. cold milk
6-oz. pkg. instant vanilla
   pudding mix
11-oz. pkg vanilla wafers,
   divided

3 ripe bananas, sliced and
   divided
8-oz. container frozen whipped
   topping, thawed

Pour milk into a large bowl and add pudding mix; beat with an electric mixer on medium-low speed for 2 minutes. Let stand for 5 minutes. Meanwhile, layer half of vanilla wafers in an ungreased 13"x9" glass baking pan. Spoon half of prepared pudding over wafers; arrange half of sliced bananas on top. Repeat layering. Spread with whipped topping. Cover and refrigerate for 3 hours, or until ready to serve. Makes 6 servings.

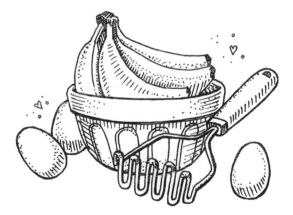

Chocolate lovers will love this quick chocolate mousse. Combine 1-1/2 cups cold milk and a 4-ounce package of instant chocolate pudding mix; whisk for 2 minutes. Fold in a 16-ounce container of thawed whipped topping until blended. Cover and chill before serving. Scrumptious!

Cherry & Pineapple Cake

Irene Robinson
Cincinnati, OH

This dessert tastes wonderful, and it's very easy to make!
I like to make it for Christmas, Valentine's Day, the 4th of July...
any holiday with a red theme.

21-oz. can cherry pie filling
15-1/4 oz. can crushed
   pineapple, drained
18-1/2 pkg. yellow cake mix
1/2 c. butter, melted

1/2 c. margarine, melted
1 c. chopped pecans
Garnish: whipped cream or
   vanilla ice cream

In a greased 13"x9" baking pan, layer all ingredients except garnish in the order listed. Do not stir. Bake at 350 degrees for 50 minutes, or until set. Garnish as desired. Makes 8 to 10 servings.

"Fried" ice cream is a fun ending to a Mexican meal. Roll scoops
of ice cream in a mixture of crushed frosted corn flakes
and cinnamon. Add a drizzle of honey and a dollop
of whipped topping. Yummy!

Speedy Cookies & Desserts

Strawberry Lemonade Ice Cream Pie

Terri Steffes
Saint Charles, MO

Whenever I have guests over to enjoy our front porch and the view of the lake, I make this pie. It's very popular, and super-easy to make.

1/2 gal. vanilla ice cream
0.19-oz. pkg. unsweetened
  strawberry lemonade
  drink mix

9-inch graham cracker crust
Garnish: whipped topping, fresh
  strawberries

Transfer ice cream to a large bowl; let stand until softened. Sprinkle drink mix over ice cream and stir gently. Spoon mixture into crust. Cover and freeze for at least one hour. Shortly before serving time, remove pie from freezer; let stand at room temperature for 8 to 10 minutes. Top with whipped topping and strawberries. Cut into wedges and serve. Makes 8 servings.

So-Easy Lemon Cheesecake

Linda Belon
Wintersville, OH

A cool, not-too-sweet dessert...good on hot summer days.

8-oz. pkg. cream cheese,
  softened
2 c. milk, divided

3.4-oz. pkg. instant lemon
  pudding mix
9-inch graham cracker crust

Combine cream cheese and 1/2 cup milk in a bowl; beat with an electric mixer on low speed until smooth and creamy. Add pudding mix and remaining milk; beat on low speed for one to 2 minutes. Spoon into pie crust. Cover and chill; cut into wedges. Serves 6 to 8.

Save calories in recipes calling for cream cheese...
choose creamy Neufchâtel cheese with 1/3 less fat instead.

Italian Christmas Cookies

Sandy Ward
Anderson, IN

Make these tasty little treats anytime as an easy pick-me-up.

16-1/2 oz. pkg. refrigerated
   sugar cookie dough
1/2 c. cream cheese, softened
1/2 c. all-purpose flour

3/4 t. almond or vanilla extract
Optional: orange, lemon or
   lime zest

Place cookie dough in a large bowl; let stand until softened and crumble. Stir in cream cheese, flour and extract until well blended. Shape dough into 1-1/4 inch balls. Arrange balls on ungreased baking sheets. Bake at 350 degrees for 11 to 13 minutes, until set on the edges. Cool on baking sheets for one minute; remove cookies to wire racks and cool completely, about 30 minutes. Dip tops of cookies into Glaze. Sprinkle with citrus zest, if desired. Keep refrigerated in an airtight container. Makes 3-1/2 dozen.

Glaze:

2-1/4 c. powdered sugar

3 to 4 T. orange, lemon or
lime juice

Mix together powdered sugar and citrus juice until smooth.

Refrigerated cookie dough is a great shortcut for all kinds of delicious homemade cookies. Add the chilled dough to a bowl and let stand for 10 to 15 minutes, then break it up and mix in add-ins by hand.

Speedy Cookies & Desserts

Peanut Butter Cookie Bars

Jessica Kraus
Delaware, OH

Super simple and delicious...why not make a batch today?

18-1/4 oz. pkg. yellow cake mix
2 eggs, beaten
1/3 c. water

1/4 c. butter, softened
1 c. creamy peanut butter
10-oz. pkg. peanut butter chips

Combine all ingredients in a large bowl; mix well. Spoon batter into a greased 13"x9" baking pan and smooth out. Bake at 350 degrees for 30 minutes. Cool; cut into bars. Makes 2 dozen.

Chocolate Chip Cookie Bars

Pam Hooley
LaGrange, IN

When the work starts outside, I need to have shortcuts in the kitchen. These yummy bars are a good substitute for cookies.

18-1/4 oz. pkg. yellow cake mix
2 eggs, beaten
1/2 c. butter, melted
1 t. vanilla extract

1/2 t. salt
6-oz. pkg. semi-sweet chocolate
  chips

In a large bowl, mix together all ingredients well. Spread batter in a greased 13"x9" baking pan. Bake at 350 degrees for 20 to 25 minutes. Cool; cut into bars. Makes about 1-1/2 dozen.

For a sweet & salty treat that's ready in moments, serve a tub of caramel apple dip with crunchy apple slices and mini pretzel twists. Yum...dig in!

Butterscotch Ice Cream Dessert

Janis Parr
Ontario, Canada

This quick & easy dessert is a big hit with everyone! Use any flavor of ice cream and sundae sauce that you like. Yummy!

1/2 c. butter
1 c. brown sugar, packed
1/2 t. vanilla extract
2-1/2 c. crispy rice cereal
Optional: 1/2 c. finely
    chopped pecans

1 qt. butterscotch ripple ice
    cream, softened
1/2 c. butterscotch sundae sauce

In a large saucepan over medium heat, combine butter and brown sugar. Cook until butter melts, stirring well. Mix in vanilla; stir in cereal and pecans, if using. Pack half of mixture into an ungreased 9"x9" baking pan; cool. Spoon ice cream on top and spread evenly. Top with remaining cereal mixture; cover and freeze. At serving time, drizzle with sundae sauce; cut into squares. Return any leftovers to the freezer. Makes 8 servings.

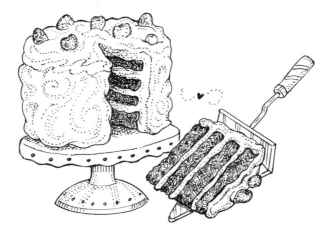

Need a special cake for a special occasion? Bake up your favorite
2-layer cake mix; cool and split the layers. Stack on a pretty
cake plate, with fluffy whipped topping in between and on top.
Add fresh berries and more topping...voilà!

Fudge Brownie Supreme

Vicki Van Donselaar
Cedar, IA

The name of this recipe doesn't do it justice. These brownies are so delicious, you won't be able to just eat one!

18-oz. pkg. brownie mix
7-oz. jar marshmallow creme
6-oz. pkg. semi-sweet
   chocolate chips

1/2 c. creamy peanut butter
2 c. crispy rice cereal

Prepare brownie mix according to package directions; pour batter into a greased 9"x9" baking pan and bake as directed. Meanwhile, scoop marshmallow creme into a microwave-safe bowl; microwave for 10 to 15 seconds, until spreadable. Spread over warm brownies. In another microwave-safe bowl, combine chocolate chips and peanut butter; microwave for 30 seconds; stir. Microwave another 20 to 25 seconds; stir until melted and smooth. Stir in cereal and spread over marshmallow creme. Cool; cut into squares. Makes 15 brownies.

For a scrumptious dessert in a jiffy, make an ice cream pie! Soften 2 pints of your favorite ice cream and spread in a graham cracker crust, then freeze. Garnish with whipped topping and cookie crumbs or fresh berries...the combinations are endless.

Best Banana Bundt Cake

Sandra Turner
Fayetteville, NC

This is my go-to recipe whenever I have ripe bananas to use up. The convenience of using boxed cake and pudding mixes along with a few kitchen staples, and mixing it all in one bowl, makes it a winner all the way around. We enjoy slices of this cake topped with fresh fruit and whipped topping...so luscious!

18-1/4 oz. pkg. yellow cake mix
3.4-oz. pkg. instant banana
   cream pudding mix
4 eggs, lightly beaten

1 c. water
1/4 c. oil
2 very ripe bananas, mashed

In a large bowl, combine dry cake and pudding mixes; stir to loosen any lumps. Add eggs, water and oil; stir to mix well. Fold in bananas. Pour batter into a greased and floured Bundt® pan. Bake at 350 degrees for 35 to 45 minutes, until a toothpick inserted in the center comes out clean. Do not overbake. Cool cake completely in pan on a wire rack; turn out onto a cake plate. Slice and serve. Makes 12 servings.

A handy trick for greasing and flouring cake pans!
Grease the pan, sprinkle with flour, cover with
plastic wrap and give it a good shake!

Speedy Cookies & Desserts

Pineapple Freeze

Rene Brooks
Donora, PA

I served this after Easter Sunday dinner. It's a light cool dessert, especially after a heavy meal...very refreshing. It can be made several days in advance.

21-oz. can pineapple pie filling
8-oz. can crushed pineapple, drained
8-oz. container sour cream
8-oz. container frozen whipped topping, thawed

Optional: 3/4 c. finely chopped pecans
Garnish: whipped cream, fresh berries

In a large bowl, mix all ingredients except garnish. Spoon into an aluminum foil-lined 9"x5" loaf pan. Cover and freeze until ready to serve. At serving time, slice and garnish with whipped cream and fresh berries. Makes 8 to 10 servings.

Banana Whoopie Cookies

Lisa Ashton
Aston, PA

I started off with a box of cake mix and decided to see what would happen. These turned out great! The cookies are soft and tasty.

18-1/2 oz. pkg. devil's food cake mix
1/3 c. oil

2 eggs, beaten
1 ripe banana, mashed
Garnish: coarse sugar

Mix dry cake mix, oil and eggs in a large bowl until a soft dough forms. Add banana; mix well. Drop dough by teaspoonfuls onto ungreased baking sheets, 2 inches apart. Sprinkle with coarse sugar. Bake at 350 degrees for 8 to 10 minutes. Cool cookies on baking sheets; they will rise and then deflate as they cool. Remove from baking sheets to a wire rack. Makes 4 dozen.

Applesauce is a tasty substitute for oil
in cookie and cake recipes.

203

Mom's Apple Kuchen

Cassie Hooker
La Porte, TX

My mom likes to make this scrumptious dessert for get-togethers, housewarming parties and baby showers. It's always a favorite.

18-1/4 oz. pkg. yellow cake mix
1/2 c. butter
1/2 c. flaked coconut
20-oz. can sliced apples,
  well drained

1/2 c. sugar
1 t. cinnamon
1 c. sour cream
2 egg yolks or 1 whole egg,
  beaten

Add dry cake mix to a large bowl; cut in butter until crumbly. Mix in coconut. Pat mixture lightly into an ungreased 13"x9" baking pan, building up the edges a little. Bake at 350 degrees for 10 minutes; remove from oven. Arrange apple slices on warm crust. Mix together sugar and cinnamon in a cup; sprinkle over apples. In a small bowl, blend together sour cream and egg yolks or egg; drizzle over apples. Topping will not completely cover apples. Bake at 350 degrees for another 25 minutes, or until edges are golden. Do not overbake. Cut into squares; serve warm. Cover and refrigerate any leftovers. Makes 12 servings.

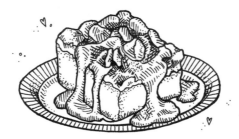

Warm caramel ice cream topping makes a delightful drizzle
over hot apple desserts. Just heat it in the microwave for
a few seconds, and it's ready to spoon over desserts.

Speedy Cookies & Desserts

Momma's Pineapple Cookies

Patty Fosnight
Martinsville, IN

My momma's trademark cookie. She created the recipe to have something different, and it soon became a family favorite, especially Dad's. You can mix up a glaze with powdered sugar and a spoonful of the pineapple juice to drizzle over the cookies...but really, they're great just the way they are!

17-1/2 oz. pkg. sugar cookie mix
1/2 c. butter, softened
1 egg, beaten
1/2 to 3/4 c. chopped pecans

15-1/4 oz. can crushed
    pineapple, drained and
    squeezed dry

In a large bowl, combine sugar cookie mix, butter and egg; mix well. Stir in pecans and pineapple. Drop dough by teaspoonfuls onto parchment paper-lined baking sheets. Bake at 350 degrees for about 12 to 14 minutes. Remove to a wire rack; cool. Makes 2 dozen.

Company on the way? A frozen pound cake topped with a can of fruit pie filling and whipped topping makes a simple and delicious dessert in minutes! Serve slices on your prettiest china.

Caramel Brownies

Lisa Burns
Findlay, OH

These gooey caramel brownies are delicious served warm, topped with a scoop of ice cream. Add a drizzle of chocolate syrup and a sprinkle of nuts for an extra-special dessert!

24 caramels, unwrapped
5-oz. can evaporated milk,
   divided
18-1/2 oz. pkg. chocolate
   cake mix

6 T. butter, melted
1 c. walnuts, coarsely chopped
1/2 c. semi-sweet chocolate chips

Combine caramels and 2 tablespoons evaporated milk in a heavy saucepan. Cook over medium heat until caramels are melted, stirring often; remove from heat. Meanwhile, in a large bowl, combine dry cake mix, butter, remaining milk and nuts; mix well. Spread half of batter in a greased 13"x9" baking pan. Bake at 350 degrees for 10 minutes. Remove from oven; sprinkle with chocolate chips and drizzle with melted caramel. Drop remaining batter over caramel layer by tablespoonfuls. Bake an additional 20 to 25 minutes; top layer will be soft. Cut into squares while still warm. Makes 1-1/2 to 2 dozen.

Add a teaspoon or 2 of espresso powder or instant coffee granules to your brownie batter...it really brings out a rich chocolate flavor.

Speedy Cookies & Desserts

Exceptional Cake Mix Cookie Bars

Jenna Harmon
Dolores, CO

We love sweet treats in our family, and also love to build cookie baskets to give away to friends, family and others in the community. Ever since I was in college, I have loved cake mixes and the versatility of everything you can bake just from one box! These cake bars are yummy, done in less than 30 minutes from start to finish and use only four ingredients! Mix it up by trying different flavors of cake mixes and chocolate add-ins.

15-1/4 oz. pkg. white cake mix
2 eggs, beaten
1/2 c. butter, melted

12-oz. pkg. semi-sweet chocolate chips

In a large bowl, mix together dry cake mix, eggs and melted butter. Batter will be thick. Fold in chocolate chips. Spread batter in a greased 13"x9" baking pan. Bake at 350 degrees for 20 to 25 minutes. Cool before cutting into bars. Makes one dozen.

Line baking sheets and pans with parchment paper cut to fit.
Cakes and cookies won't stick, and clean-up is oh-so easy.

Crispy Lemon Cookies

Jackie Smulski
Lyons, IL

I love the light crisp texture of these cookies...it's a great complement to the burst of lemon tanginess. Serve with a cold glass of lemonade or iced tea.

18-1/4 oz. pkg. lemon cake mix
1 c. crispy rice cereal
1/2 c. butter, melted

1 egg, beaten
2 t. lemon zest

Combine all ingredients in a large bowl; stir until thoroughly mixed. Dough will be crumbly. Shape into one-inch balls. Place on ungreased baking sheets, 2 inches apart. Bake at 350 degrees for 10 to 12 minutes, until lightly golden. Cool on baking sheets for 5 minutes; remove to a wire rack. Makes 4 dozen.

Angel Food Delight

Paula Marchesi
Auburn, PA

I make this delicious dessert every Memorial Day. It's quick & easy, and you can change your choice of fruit.

1 pt. vanilla ice cream, softened
1 c. milk
3.4-oz. pkg. instant vanilla
   pudding mix

1 pt. strawberries, hulled
   and sliced
1 angel food cake, sliced

In a large bowl, combine ice cream and milk; blend well. Add dry pudding mix; stir for one minute, or until well blended. Fold in strawberries. Cover and refrigerate until thickened. At serving time, spoon over slices of angel food cake. Serves 8 to 10.

Keep ingredients on hand for a yummy, quick-fix dessert.
A real life-saver whenever your child announces,
"Mom, there's a bake sale...tomorrow!"

Speedy Cookies & Desserts

Raspberry Cookie Bars

Lori Rosenberg
Cleveland, OH

A favorite cookie alternative for those who don't care for chocolate.
Try it with another favorite flavor of jam, too!

18-oz. pkg. refrigerated sugar
   cookie dough, softened
3/4 t. almond extract

1/2 c. seedless raspberry jam
1/4 c. chopped pecans

Line an 8"x8" glass baking pan with foil, creating 2-inch "handles" on 2 sides. Spray with non-stick vegetable spray; set aside. In a large bowl, combine cookie dough and extract; knead to combine. With moistened fingers, press 2/3 of dough into the bottom of pan. Spread jam over dough. Crumble remaining dough evenly over jam; sprinkle with pecans. Bake at 350 degrees for 30 to 35 minutes, until center is set and edges are golden. Let cool in pan. Lift cookie bars out of pan, using the foil handles; cut into squares. Makes 1-1/2 dozen.

Jars of jam and preserves make great souvenirs when on family vacations. Later, use them to bake up jam bars or thumbprints... the flavors will bring back happy memories!

Easy Gingerbread Cookies

Lynnette Jones
East Flat Rock, NC

These are my family's favorite cookies. Good for dessert or with afternoon coffee or tea.

15-1/4 oz. pkg. spice cake mix
3/4 c. all-purpose flour
2 eggs, beaten
1/3 c. oil

1/3 c. molasses
2 t. ground ginger
Garnish: candy sprinkles
    or raisins

In a large bowl, combine dry cake mix and remaining ingredients except garnish; mix well. Cover and refrigerate for 30 minutes, until dough is well chilled. Roll out dough on a floured surface; cut into desired shapes with cookie cutters. Arrange cookies on ungreased baking sheets. Decorate with sprinkles or raisins, as desired. Bake at 375 degrees for 8 to 11 minutes, until edges are set. Cool on wire racks. Makes 2-1/2 dozen.

When rolling out cookie dough, sprinkle powdered sugar on the work surface. So much tastier than using flour, and it works just as well!

Speedy Cookies & Desserts

Chocolate Cluster Cookies

Erin Brock
Charleston, WV

Yummy and oh-so easy to make! I like to change out the candy-coated chocolates to go with the season, like red and green for Christmas or orange and brown for Halloween.

18-oz. pkg. refrigerated sugar
   cookie dough, softened
1/3 c. creamy peanut butter
1/2 c. semi-sweet chocolate chips

1/2 c. candy-coated chocolates
1/2 c. old-fashioned oats,
   uncooked

Transfer dough to a large bowl; let stand until softened. Mix in peanut butter. Add chocolate chips, candies and oats; mix well. Drop dough by tablespoons onto greased baking sheets, 3 inches apart. Bake at 375 degrees for 10 to 12 minutes, until lightly golden. Cool on baking sheets for one minute. Remove to a wire rack and cool completely. Makes 2 dozen.

Surprise everyone with cookie-stuffed brownie cups! Drop chocolate sandwich cookies into greased muffin cups, one to a cup. Fill 2/3 full with brownie batter. Bake at 350 degrees for 20 minutes, or until a toothpick comes out with a few crumbs sticking to it. Cool and serve.

Best Berry Brownie Pizza

Paula Marchesi
Auburn, PA

*Bet you can't resist this pizza for dessert! This is one great way to
make the most of fresh summer berries, which are delicious with
a brownie crust. I've been making it for quite a few years.*

18-oz. pkg. fudge brownie mix
1-1/4 c. cold milk
3.4-oz. pkg. instant pudding mix
2-1/2 c. frozen whipped topping,
   thawed

2 c. assorted fresh berries
Garnish: chocolate syrup,
   chopped pecans

Prepare brownie mix according to package direction; spread batter
onto a greased 12" round pizza pan. Bake at 350 degrees for 18 to
22 minutes, until a toothpick inserted near the center comes out almost
clean. Set pan on a wire rack; cool for 15 to 20 minutes. Meanwhile, in
a bowl, whisk together milk and pudding mix for 2 minutes. Let stand
for 2 minutes, or until soft-set. Fold in whipped topping; spread over
brownie crust. Top with berries. Drizzle chocolate syrup over berries;
sprinkle with pecans. Cover and refrigerate until chilled. Cut into wedges
or squares and serve. Makes 12 servings.

If a baked dessert didn't turn out quite right, layer it with whipped
cream in a parfait glass and give it a fancy name. It will still be
scrumptious...and nobody will know the difference!

Speedy Cookies & Desserts

Baked Crescent Churros

Rita Morgan
Pueblo, CO

Let the kids help make these...perfect for a Taco Tuesday treat!

2 T. sugar
1 t. cinnamon
8-oz. tube refrigerated
    crescent rolls

2 T. butter, melted

Mix sugar and cinnamon in a cup; set aside. Unroll dough; separate into 4 rectangles. Press each into a 6-inch by 4-inch rectangle; press perforations to seal. Brush melted butter over 2 rectangles; sprinkle with half of cinnamon-sugar mixture. Top each with a remaining rectangle; press edges lightly. Brush tops with melted butter. Cut each lengthwise into 6 strips. Twist each strip 3 times; place on an ungreased baking sheet. Bake at 375 degrees for 9 to 11 minutes, until crisp and golden. Brush with any remaining butter; sprinkle with remaining cinnamon-sugar and serve. Makes one dozen.

Speedy Snickerdoodles

Lisanne Miller
Manitoba, Canada

This is a great cookie recipe to make with children! It is the first cookie we make for the holiday season and always a favorite. It's updated by using a yellow cake mix, for less fuss and great flavor.

1/4 c. cinnamon
1/4 c. sugar
18-1/2 oz. pkg. yellow cake mix

2 eggs, beaten
1/4 c. oil

In a plastic zipping bag, combine cinnamon and sugar. Shake to mix well and set aside. In a large bowl, combine dry cake mix, eggs and oil. With an electric mixer on medium speed, beat well until a firm dough forms. Do not mix by hand. Form dough into walnut-size balls. Add balls to cinnamon-sugar in bag; shake until coated. Place on parchment paper-lined baking sheets. Bake at 350 degrees for 15 to 18 minutes. Makes 3-1/2 dozen.

Easy Key Lime Pie

Irene Robinson
Cincinnati, OH

This dessert will make you think you're in Key West, Florida! Save time by using a store-bought graham cracker crust; bake as directed.

4 egg yolks, lightly beaten,
   room temperature
14-oz. can sweetened
   condensed milk

1/2 c. Key lime juice
Garnish: whipped cream,
   fresh berries

Prepare and bake Graham Cracker Crust; set aside to cool. Meanwhile, beat egg yolks in a large bowl. Add condensed milk and lime juice; whisk together well. Pour into pie crust. Bake at 350 degrees for 20 to 25 minutes, until center looks set but is still wobbly. Cover and refrigerate at least one hour before slicing. Garnish slices with whipped cream and berries. Serves 6 to 8.

Graham Cracker Crust:

1-1/2 c. graham crackers,
   crushed

1/4 c. sugar
6 T. butter, melted

Combine all ingredients; mix well and pat into a 9" pie plate. Bake at 350 degrees for 7 to 10 minutes, to desired crispness. Cool.

When the recipe calls for cracker crumbs, seal crackers in
a plastic zipping bag, then crush with a rolling pin. No mess!

Speedy Cookies & Desserts

Cherry Ice Cream Sensation

Marlene Burns
Cedar Rapids, IA

I make this recipe as a treat for summertime birthday parties.

10 ice cream sandwiches
21-oz. can cherry pie filling
12-oz. container frozen whipped
    topping, thawed

Garnish: chocolate sprinkles

Arrange ice cream sandwiches in a single layer in an ungreased 13"x9" baking pan. Spread pie filling evenly over sandwiches; spread evenly with whipped topping. Top with sprinkles. Cover and freeze for 4 hours, or until firm. Remove from freezer 10 minutes before serving; cut into bars. Return any leftovers to the freezer. Makes 12 servings.

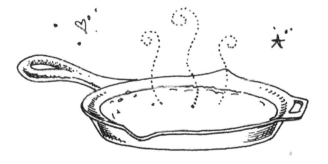

Bake up a skillet cookie! Pat a tube of refrigerated sugar cookie dough into a cast-iron skillet. Bake at 350 degrees for 40 to 45 minutes, until golden on top and lightly golden on the edges. The cookie will continue to bake for a few minutes out of the oven. Turn onto a wire rack to cool slightly and cut into wedges. Yummy!

Pudding & Pineapple Cake

Debbie Benzi
Binghamton, NY

A coworker brought this cake to work many times to celebrate office birthdays. She gave me the recipe and I've made it for many family birthdays...it's always a hit! Make a scrumptious variation by using chocolate cake mix, chocolate pudding and ripe bananas.

18-1/2 oz. pkg. yellow cake mix
8-oz. pkg. cream cheese,
   softened
1 c. milk
3.4-oz. pkg. instant vanilla
   pudding mix

15-1/4 oz. can crushed
   pineapple, drained
8-oz. container frozen whipped
   topping, thawed

Prepare cake mix according to package directions; bake in a greased 13"x9" baking pan. Cool completely. Meanwhile, in a large bowl, beat cream cheese until soft. Add milk and dry pudding mix; stir together until well blended and spread over cake. Spread pineapple over pudding mixture. Spread whipped topping over pineapple; cover and refrigerate. Cut into squares to serve. Makes 12 servings.

Keep plastic wrap from sticking to frosting when you're transporting a dessert. Stick mini marshmallows on the ends of toothpicks. Stick the other end of each toothpick into the cake. Gently cover with plastic wrap...no sticking, and the toothpicks won't poke holes through the wrap!

Audrey's Apple Streusel

Audrey Szostak
Elma, NY

Old-fashioned goodness, but so simple to make. Perfect with a cup of coffee or tea.

18-1/2 oz. pkg. yellow cake mix
2 eggs, beaten
1/2 t. lemon extract
21-oz. can apple pie filling

1/2 c. all-purpose flour
1/2 c. sugar
1/2 t. cinnamon
1/4 c. butter, melted

In a large bowl, mix together dry cake mix, eggs and extract; stir in pie filling. Pour batter into a greased 13"x9" baking pan. In another bowl, mix together remaining ingredients with a fork until crumbly. Sprinkle over batter. Bake at 350 degrees for 42 to 47 minutes, until golden. Cut into squares. Makes 12 to 15 servings.

Whipped cream is a must with homemade desserts.
Save time...pick up an aerosol can of sweetened
whipped cream and dollop away!

INDEX

INDEX

Find Gooseberry Patch
wherever you are!

www.gooseberrypatch.com

Email

Call us toll-free at 1·800·854·6673

aPRONS · SUNDAY DINNER · ROLLING PINS

ReUNioNS

HaNDeD · DOWN ReCiPes

starched

Cream Gravy

sweet Memories

warm Hugs · scrapbooks · Tried & True

U.S. to Metric Recipe Equivalents

Volume Measurements

1/4 teaspoon	1 mL
1/2 teaspoon	2 mL
1 teaspoon	5 mL
1 tablespoon = 3 teaspoons	15 mL
2 tablespoons = 1 fluid ounce	30 mL
1/4 cup	60 mL
1/3 cup	75 mL
1/2 cup = 4 fluid ounces	125 mL
1 cup = 8 fluid ounces	250 mL
2 cups = 1 pint =16 fluid ounces	500 mL
4 cups = 1 quart	1 L

Weights

1 ounce	30 g
4 ounces	120 g
8 ounces	225 g
16 ounces = 1 pound	450 g

Oven Temperatures

300° F	150° C
325° F	160° C
350° F	180° C
375° F	190° C
400° F	200° C
450° F	230° C

Baking Pan Sizes

Square

8x8x2 inches	2 L = 20x20x5 cm
9x9x2 inches	2.5 L = 23x23x5 cm

Rectangular

13x9x2 inches	3.5 L = 33x23x5 cm

Loaf

9x5x3 inches	2 L = 23x13x7 cm

Round

8x1-1/2 inches	1.2 L = 20x4 cm
9x1-1/2 inches	1.5 L = 23x4 cm